Here's to Your
Passion Capital.!!

[signature]

The WORLD'S
MOST VALUABLE ASSET

PASSION
CAPITAL

PAUL ALOFS

SIGNAL
McCLELLAND
& STEWART

Library and Archives Canada Cataloguing in Publication

Alofs, Paul
Passion capital : the world's most valuable asset / Paul Alofs.

ISBN 978-0-7710-0747-7

1. Success in business. I. Title.

HF5386.A586 2012   650.1   C2011-907955-0

We acknowledge the financial support of the Government of Canada through
the Canada Book Fund and that of the Government of Ontario through the
Ontario Media Development Corporation's Ontario Book Initiative. We further
acknowledge the support of the Canada Council for the Arts and the
Ontario Arts Council for our publishing program.

Library of Congress Control Number: 2011945921

Typeset in Electra by M&S, Toronto

Printed and bound in the United States of America

McClelland & Stewart Ltd.
75 Sherbourne Street
Toronto, Ontario
M5A 2P9
www.mcclelland.com

1 2 3 4 5   16 15 14 13 12

This book is dedicated to the late Mrs. Pat Alofs,
who was the original passion capitalist in my life.

CON⊤

PREFACE

WE LIVE IN THE "GOOGLE WORLD." We can go to Google and instantly get the answer to just about any question.

In the Google world, answers and information are commodities. In a world full of answers, the value resides in asking the right questions.

This book is about a question. That question has to do with the meaning and measure of value. In a world of false prosperity created by easy credit and massive debt, it is difficult to assess what is of value. In this climate of uncertainty, what is truly our most valuable asset? What asset is dependable, investable, and sustainable?

In short, *what is the world's most valuable asset?*

This is not just a question to me. It has become a profound obsession. The question is both simple and complex. In lighter moments I call it my "beach ball question." Have you ever inflated a beach ball and tried to hold it under water? You can't, at least not for long. Eventually the beach ball springs to the surface. A beach ball question is one you can't hold down.

My research laboratory for answering this question is a career spent in leadership roles in the private sector and the not-for-profit sector. The answer to this question has been shaped by my working in top international companies and for one of the world's top cancer research hospitals. The observations, stories, and insights are gained from the real world and from a career of significant breadth and depth. They come from both victory and defeat.

I have spent more than twenty years considering this question, and it has taken me two years of challenging work to answer it with this book.

This book is meant to inform and stimulate and to answer the question, "What is the world's most valuable asset?" The answer will surprise you.

Passion Capital demonstrates how and why some companies have risen to the top of their sector and others have failed. It explains the fallen fortunes of America and the rising economies of China and India. There are lessons not just for business but for careers, causes, and countries.

This book explains transformation, and it shows you how to embrace this transformation. It explains why passion capital is the world's most valuable asset and it gives you the tools you need to discover, build, and succeed with passion capital.

Passion Capital explores a brand-new asset class, one that is vital to your success. Read this book and you will never look at your career, company, cause, or country the same way.

ALICE COOPER, SUN TZU, AND

A NEW WORLD ORDER

IT WAS JULY 5, 1991, AND ALICE COOPER was on the roof of the HMV store on Toronto's Yonge Street getting ready for his three-song set. He was wearing his horror-film makeup, in character. I was the thirty-five-year-old president of HMV Canada, and a lifelong fan. Cooper talked briefly about his golf game, and I thanked him for his impromptu performance. I was a bit worried we'd be shut down; I hadn't applied for a permit for the concert because I knew we wouldn't get one. Below us, thousands of fans were loudly waiting. Beside me, a few employees were throwing down HMV discount coupons attached to two-dollar bills. It looked like a thunderstorm was approaching from the west. Alice wrapped up his golf conversation and tore into his first song, "Under My Wheels." The crowd went wild, and for fifteen minutes Yonge Street was jammed by good-natured civil disobedience.

Cooper's performance confirmed that our flagship store was a success. We'd been open for only two months, but we sold more CDs on opening day than we had projected for our first week. It was also a personal validation for me. HMV was a successful music retailer in England, and the Yonge Street store was the beginning of its expansion across Canada and into other international markets. The opening of this store was critical to the chain, and critical to my career.

One of my worries was that I had no experience in retail management. I had come from an enterprise called Electronic Marketing Systems that was visionary in its product but confused in its technology. As a result it was a colossal failure. At the time, Canada was one of the most densely saturated retail music markets in the world, and Yonge Street was the epicentre of the national industry. Steps away were the two kings of record retailing, Sam the Record Man, owned by the venerable Sam Sniderman, and the flagship store of a solid, well-managed chain, A&A Records. Across the street was Sunrise Records. In the Eaton Centre, which Alice Cooper could see from the HMV roof, were a few more record stores. We were number six in a market with six major retailers.

HMV didn't want to find a place in this market. It wanted to conquer it, as unlikely as that seemed. I had been given the task.

The first thing I did when I joined the company was buy a copy of Sun Tzu's *The Art of War*. One of the lessons in that book is: Pretend to be weak. So I already had an advantage: the competition already thought I was weak. Sam Sniderman had told the press that I didn't know what I was doing and both the store and I would be gone in a year.

In any battle it is imperative to know your enemy. Sam the Record Man was a local legend. It was three storeys of sloping floors and eclectic product, a maze of record bins. It tended to be staffed by band members who expressed contempt if you didn't know the guitar tuning on the second cut of side two of an early Ry Cooder album. It was a place for aficionados. A&A was more corporate, better organized, less idiosyncratic. Between these two poles there didn't seem to be much territory left to occupy. Early on I identified my chief competitors' respective strengths and weaknesses. I recognized the managerial strength of A&A and hired away their manager. (*If his forces are united, separate them*, wrote Sun Tzu.)

After assessing their stores' physical layout, I realized that we could design a better store than either of them. I was given the job of designing the HMV store and poured my heart into it. My first attempt was rejected, but I went back with renewed vigour. I visited some of the world's great record stores – Tower Records on Sunset Boulevard in West Hollywood, the HMV flagship on London's Oxford Street, and Virgin's first megastore, also on Oxford Street – and studied what they had done. One thing they had in common was that they were perceived not just as retail stores but as destinations. They were like an endless, well-managed party.

My next design was airy, bright, and well-organized – the opposite of Sam's. It was so successful that I was given the job of leading the HMV store design globally.

In our Yonge Street store we installed five hundred listening posts, a DJ booth, a stage for live performances, and what was the largest video wall in Canada at the time – thirty-six screens mounted outside and angled toward the sidewalk – and it stopped traffic. We had aggressive pricing and the largest inventory in the country. We kept an ear to the ground for any trend that was breaking. Local DJs quickly chose our store to do their shopping.

I started hiring staff six months before we opened. They were well trained and came from outside the ranks of deeply knowledgeable contemptuous garage-band fanatics. I distributed copies of *The Art of War* to all the senior managers (*He will win whose army is animated by the same spirit throughout the ranks*). I implemented an inventory system whereby individual store managers could buy for the specific needs or tastes of their clientele (*He will win who has military capacity and is not interfered with by the sovereign*). However, this independence was backstopped by a computer program that tracked how successful their decisions were. So there was both flexibility and accountability.

Within three years we were number one in the Canadian market, going from selling $28 million to $200 million worth of music and merchandise; one of every five CDs sold in Canada was sold through our stores. When the digital music revolution finally came, HMV was the last chain left standing.

You might ask how a guy in his early thirties with no experience in retail management and who had just come out of a disastrous business venture was given the job of president of a national chain. There were moments I wondered that myself. But my immediate boss, Stuart McAllister, saw something in me, something I was beginning to see myself on that rooftop with Alice Cooper. The quality that he saw was passion. Passion with a plan.

It was from this early experience that I began to form the ideas behind "passion capital."

———

If you were to ask CEOs what their company's most valuable asset is, they might reply that it was their people, or perhaps their customers. They might say it was intellectual capital, or financial capital, or even social capital. All of these are valuable assets, but none are as valuable as *passion* capital.

The value of passion capital is that it is the foundation upon which all other forms of capital are built. With passion capital, you can acquire the others.

Expressed as a formula, passion capital looks like this:

Passion Capital = Energy + Intensity + Sustainability

This book is the result of a lifetime of circling around this single idea: what is the world's most valuable asset? What is it that makes some businesses successful while many others fail? What differentiates individuals who succeed from those who don't? One of the benefits of having spent years wrestling with this question is that it provided me with a long-term perspective. People who seemed like bright lights eventually burned out. What seemed like a brilliant idea eventually faded (the much-hyped Segway comes to mind). I wanted to know what worked in the long term. How do you sustain a good idea?

It was clear that passion was at the base of so many successful enterprises. But passion, as we know, can be fleeting. How did people sustain their passion? What qualities allowed this passion to be not just the animating spark but the sustaining drive in an enterprise?

Over time, I broadened my scope. It wasn't just businesses I looked at, but politics, sports, philanthropy. I examined countries and causes and sought to identify what worked and what didn't and why it didn't. I've included many examples in this book of passion capitalists – people and companies that exemplify a quality that is necessary for passion capital.

You probably instinctively recognize some passion capitalists already. Steve Jobs was one, certainly. John Lasseter, co-founder of Pixar. Isadore Sharp, founder of the Four Seasons chain of hotels. Oprah Winfrey is a passion capitalist, as was Golda Meir. Ken Thomson; Warren Buffett; T. Boone Pickens; Guy Laliberté, the founder of Cirque du Soleil; and John Mackey, who started Whole Foods. They are all passion capitalists.

And you can be one too.

This is a diverse group of people with diverse beliefs. But each of them could very likely define his or her core beliefs. Many of them believed in something that few others did at the time. John Lasseter thought computer animation was the future of animated films. Disney disagreed and lost him. T. Boone Pickens, the quintessential oilman, now believes that wind and natural gas are better bets than oil for securing his nation's energy security. His former oil colleagues think he's a heretic. Steve Jobs saw a way to revolutionize the music retailing industry. All of these people and their stories are part of this book. They are part of the move toward a new way of looking at capitalism, at establishing a new blueprint for success and sustainability.

It was up on the roof with Alice Cooper that I first had the sense that I was a passion capitalist. I hadn't defined the term yet, but it was something I instinctively was drawn to. I had a passion for music, and a passion for winning. But it was only after success in other fields that I began to understand how my passion for music and my passion for winning came together. It wasn't just the successes, of course; I learned a great deal from my failures too. I also learned from the successes and failures of others. Some of those stories are in this book.

1

DEFINING PASSION CAPITAL

Without passion you don't have energy,
without energy you have nothing.
DONALD TRUMP

You can hear passion in the voice of great singers and in the music of brilliant musicians. You see it in great books, in architecture, in theatre and film. It is instantly recognizable but difficult to measure. Who was more passionate: Ella Fitzgerald or Frank Sinatra? Without that essential quality, neither of them would have been as successful as they were. But it took more than passion to sustain careers that spanned decades, that transcended musical styles and survived changes in musical taste.

Passion is an emotion, but passion capital is an asset. It is the energy, intensity, and sustainability that leaders use to build lasting value. It begins with passion, but it needs more than just emotion to sustain it. Creating passion capital means taking a strong emotion and turning it into a valuable asset.

Passion capital has an element of alchemy to it. Passion becomes purpose. Business is composed of various kinds of capital: financial, human, intellectual, and technological. The traditional idea is that when you have these elements in sufficient supply, you simply need an effective strategy to pull them together and success will come.

Yet it doesn't always. The history of business is littered with examples in which all the elements were seemingly in place and yet the enterprise failed. Why? Somehow the business failed to transform the essential idea into success. They were missing passion capital. Organizations that possess passion capital lead their sectors with the focused energy that is a hallmark of the asset. Companies that don't possess it get stuck in neutral, squander their competitive advantages, and fail to realize their potential.

Passion capital is as necessary in government as it is in business. There are governments – federal, civic, regional – that are innovative, whether in building infrastructure or fighting deficits. But as we saw with the deadlocked U.S. Congress over the issue of debt, governments can become moribund and ineffective; resources and energy are easily squandered.

When British artist Tracey Emin was invited by newly elected British prime minister David Cameron to contribute a work of art to 10 Downing Street in London, she chose something that was at odds with the often staid portraits that hang there. It was a bright neon sign that says, "More Passion." It has been quite a while since the word could be fairly applied to a British prime minister. John Major certainly didn't have it. Tony Blair began his term with it, but it disappeared. Perhaps the most passionate prime minister of the last century was Winston Churchill. Emin's installation was a loud reminder that the office would benefit from a little passion. It would be a good start, certainly.

Passion is the key to energy and energy is key to every business. It is key to life. In 1928, the Hungarian scientist Ludwig von Bertalanffy developed what he called general systems theory. All living things operate on this basic law:

Inputs → Transformation → Outputs → Feedback

For a human being, the inputs are water and food, which create energy (transformation), which is applied to survival (output). For a business, it is money and people, which go toward a strategy, which creates capital.

General systems theory is governed by a few basic laws (with apologies to von Bertalanffy – this is a simplification of his theory). The first is homeostasis, which means systems fight change. This has been my experience working with various companies. It is very hard to implement change. And it is often very necessary.

The second law is entropy – without energy, everything runs down and decays. You see it in nature, in people, and you see it in corporations.

The third law is environment – no system is self-contained. They all operate within a larger environment. Companies that aren't tuned to the environment – the markets, the competition, the consumer – are doomed.

One of the best ways to illustrate passion capital is to offer a few examples.

HAVE PASSION CAPITAL	DON'T HAVE PASSION CAPITAL
APPLE	MICROSOFT
WHOLE FOODS MARKET	GAP
CIRQUE DU SOLEIL	RINGLING BROS. CIRCUS
JOHNSON & JOHNSON	KRAFT
GOOGLE	YAHOO!
FORD	CHRYSLER
PIXAR	SONY
WAHAHA CHINA	PEPSICO
PING AN INSURANCE	AIG
FOUR SEASONS HOTELS AND RESORTS	SEARS

Listening to the Music

Being in the music business, I had a chance to meet a lot of interesting musicians. One of the most interesting was Daniel Lanois. He's released a dozen CDs but is better known as one of the most influential producers in the world. *Rolling Stone* magazine called Lanois the "most important producer to emerge in the Eighties." His credits include some of the biggest names in music (U2, Bob Dylan, Neil Young, Peter Gabriel, Willie Nelson) and some of the most successful albums of the last few decades (*The Joshua Tree*, *Achtung Baby*, *All That You Can't Leave Behind*, *Oh Mercy*, *Wrecking Ball*).

Lanois knew what he wanted to do at the age of nine, and set up a recording studio in his mother's basement in Ancaster, Ontario, at the age of seventeen. "My mother was a hairdresser with four French Canadian kids. We had no chance. I put all my efforts into music, into my talent. I put it into my passion." He recorded local artists and worked as a musician, driven by both his passion and survival instincts ("I like to be around people who get things *done*," he says). That passion has endeared him to artists. "They know I want to make a masterpiece," he says.

In 1989, Bono of U2 recommended Lanois to Bob Dylan, who had a bunch of songs he wasn't sure he wanted to record. Dylan had said he was thinking of pouring lighter fluid over the song sheets. Bono said, "No, no, you should work with Daniel Lanois." U2 had already worked with Daniel on *Unforgettable Fire* and *The Joshua Tree* and thought Dylan and Daniel would be good together. They were.

Daniel "had an extraordinary passion for music," Dylan wrote in *Chronicles*, the first volume of his autobiography. "If anybody had the light, I figured Danny did and he might turn it on. He seemed like the kind of cat who, when he works on something, he did it like the fate of the world hinged on its outcome." The result of their collaboration was *Oh Mercy*, which was a huge critical success, and a resurrection of sorts for Dylan.

"It isn't just the passion," Lanois says. "It's the values behind that passion." There still needs to be the kind of discipline and purpose that accomplish things, that put that passion to work.

Lanois says that chasing a musical trend or commercial success kills passion, and rarely ends in work of lasting value. It is ultimately cynical, resulting only in short-term gain. But work that is created out of passion often has lasting value, and as a result it can achieve commercial success and set new trends. "If you touch even one heart, then they'll tell another heart, and another," Lanois says.

Lanois is an example of a passion capitalist because he ignored musical trends and followed his own musical instincts. He was interested in a musical *life* rather than a career. His passion was infectious, and it influenced some of the greatest artists of our time and has left a musical legacy.

Passion capital creates the alchemy that is necessary for transformational success. There are seven principles which are the basis for passion capital that I have noted in a career devoted to understanding the idea. They are:

1. Creed
2. Culture
3. Courage
4. Brand
5. Resources
6. Strategy
7. Persistence

These principles are like the fuel necessary to build a fire. But you still need a spark. Passion is the spark, but without these seven principles, the fire can fail to catch, or it can burn out quickly. It is the fire that is the passion capital, that is the tangible asset.

Passion capital is what you have when the passion that begins an enterprise – whether it's a tech start-up or a term in office – is underpinned by the seven principles.

You Are What You Eat

Opening a vegetarian supermarket in beef-crazy Texas defines going against the grain. But that is what John Mackey did, in Austin in 1978, when he launched the first vegetarian supermarket in the state. He started it with $45,000 borrowed from friends and family and called it SaferWay (a direct challenge to Safeway). He lost half his money the first year, but in the second, he made a small profit of $5,000. It was enough to convince him to expand. He opened two more stores in Austin, then went into Dallas, Houston, and New Orleans. In 1980, he merged with another natural-foods store and called the new enterprise Whole Foods. In 1991, the company went public and expanded aggressively. One criterion for new locations was the number of college graduates within a sixteen-minute drive (though Mackey himself didn't graduate).

Whole Foods is today a multinational that is synonymous with organic, healthy food. There are 280 stores, with $8 billion in annual sales, and 54,000 employees. Mackey's gamble has made him a very wealthy man.

It wasn't Mackey's store that was revolutionary but the structure and scale of it. In the 1970s and '80s, thousands of small organic stores scattered across the continent were selling similar products. Instead of opening a small health food store, Mackey went big. Selling a wide range of organically produced food, his store had the same economies of scale, the same breadth of product, as Safeway or Loblaws.

The market was ready for Mackey's concept. It was prepared to pay more for organic groceries, and it welcomed his exotic selection. There was already an established niche market – often labelled tree-huggers or granola people. But there was also a quiet but growing market that was neither of those, people who wanted organic food but weren't interested in searching for small specialty stores. Whole Foods expanded out from the traditional foods and supplements that were found in those stores, merging high-end gourmet foods with organic principles and embracing local producers. It attracted a well-heeled clientele who hadn't necessarily been going to the specialty stores but would flock to an expensive supermarket. Mackey understood the demographic and their growing concern about what they ate.

The product at Whole Foods was great, but it was the brand that really caught on. Mackey turned his passion for healthy eating (he is a vegetarian) into a thriving brand. The Whole Foods brand is now so entrenched that it has entered the language as a term. The *Wall Street Journal* wrote that for the Republican Party to revitalize itself, it would have to embrace "Whole Foods Republicans," which meant conservatives with progressive lifestyles. This shorthand was instantly understood, a great thing for any brand.

Whole Foods is no longer vegetarian – it has bowed to the realities of the market and the fact that excluding carnivores in a large-scale grocery business is financial suicide. But it has held to its philosophy of selling healthful and local foods.

Mackey studied philosophy and religion at the University of Texas, and when he first went into business he did so with the idea that corporations were evil. But, he has said, "once you start meeting a payroll, you have a little different attitude about those things." He has been characterized as a right-wing hippie, someone who is a fan of Ayn Rand and Ronald

Reagan but employs a left-wing sensibility to the store and its products and its non-hierarchical management.

Whole Foods occupies only 1 per cent of the North American grocery market, yet it started a food revolution. It changed the way people shopped and ate, and it changed the way farmers grew their crops – $8 billion in sales can effect change at the supply level. Initially the large chains – Costco, Wal-Mart, Safeway – didn't really care if a former hippie found a niche with organic produce. But $8 billion is a significant niche, and Mackey's competitors have responded with their own natural and organic options.

When Mackey initially looked to expand Whole Foods, he appealed to venture capitalists. The reception wasn't warm. Of the twelve he solicited, only three agreed to meet, and they weren't encouraging. "You know, I really think you're just selling hippie food to hippies," one of them said. "I gotta tell you that I don't think it's going to work. But if it does work, Safeway's going to just steal it from you and you're not going to be able to exist anyway." Mackey was worried about Safeway and the other chains, but that didn't stop him from trying to fulfill his vision, and none of the big companies took an interest until Whole Foods had captured a large part of the organic food market.

The interest of large competitors, while a threat to his business, was at the same time a vindication of his dream. Mackey began with the strong belief that if Americans ate healthier food, they would suffer from fewer diseases like cancer, diabetes, and heart disease. Two-thirds of the country is overweight, with a third characterized as morbidly obese. If Mackey's revolution found traction, he believed those figures would drop. The stores promote a healthier life for a North American culture besieged by junk food. Mackey hoped that ultimately his stores would help alleviate the pressure on the overburdened health care system.

"Whole Foods has a deeper purpose," Mackey has said. "Most of the companies I most admire in the world have a deeper purpose."

And what is that purpose? "Business serves society," he said in a profile in the *New Yorker*. "It produces goods and services that make people's lives better. Doctors heal the sick. Teachers educate people. Architects design buildings. Whole Foods puts food on people's tables and we improve people's health. We provide jobs. We provide capital through profits that spur improvements in the world. And we're good citizens in the communities; we take our citizenship very seriously at Whole Foods." (Five per cent of profits are donated to charity.)

It isn't only the product that has a revolutionary aspect; Mackey takes one dollar a year in salary and has publicly criticized over-the-top executive compensation (which in 2010 averaged 319 times employee salaries for S&P 500 companies). At the time of writing, Whole Foods has been selected by *Fortune* magazine as one of the "100 Best Companies to Work For" every year since 1998.

When the recession hit in 2008, Whole Foods took a hit as well, though not as large as most companies. To find a way to weather the storm without losing jobs, Mackey appealed to his employees. "Whole Foods is this very empowered culture," he said, "so we unleashed the collective intelligence or the creativity of the company to find ways to cut costs." They were able to get through the difficult times with a minimum of job losses and returned to profitability the following year.

Mackey's is a passion capital story because he embodies not just the passion that began his venture but the seven principles necessary to build and sustain it. He began with a creed, developed a unique and effective culture, showed courage in going against the grain, created a brand that has entered the language, took advantage of limited resources, pursued a strategy that allowed him to dominate the market, and demonstrated persistence throughout. All of this seems obvious in retrospect, but little of it was evident at the time.

"I've met a lot of successful entrepreneurs," Mackey said. "They all started their businesses not to maximize shareholder value or money but because they were pursuing a dream."

The key to success is applying the seven principles and turning the dream into something tangible – into passion capital.

KEY LESSONS

1. Creating passion capital involves taking a strong emotion and turning it into a valuable asset. Passion capital is used to build transformational success.

2. Passion capital expressed as a formula looks like this:
   Passion Capital = Energy + Intensity + Sustainability

3. Passion capital is a brand-new asset class and the foundation upon which all other forms of capital are built. It is the alpha form of capital and is the world's most valuable asset.

4. Passion capital is created by applying seven principles: creed, culture, courage, brand, resources, strategy, and persistence.

5. A passion capitalist is a transformational leader who uses the seven principles to create passion capital for his career, company, cause, or country.

2

CREED:

THE POWER OF BELIEF

A man's action is only a picture book of his creed.
ARTHUR HELPS

M y mother died of cancer at 1 a.m. on November 2, 2002, in Windsor, Ontario. I had been taking care of her in her final weeks and I was with her when she died. Despite the late hour, I drove back to Toronto that night. On the way, I played the Beatles' "Let It Be" over and over. I must have played it twenty-five times. There was something comforting in the song. It sounded like a prayer somehow.

It wasn't until much later that I found out that Paul McCartney had been inspired to write that song after waking up from a dream about his own mother. His mother, Mary, had died of cancer when McCartney was fourteen. At a stressful time in his life, she appeared in a dream, saying to him, "It will be all right, just let it be."

"Let It Be" spoke to a lot of people; it is one of the Beatles'

I promise to do my Best,

biggest hits. It was released after the Beatles announced they were splitting up, and it resonated in the vacuum they left. The song was simple and memorable and it connected with millions of people.

When I worked in the music business, I heard a lot of songs – a few hits, a lot of misses. No one knows where hits come from. Often even the songwriter doesn't know. Hit songs can come from unexpected people or unexpected places, but two things I noticed: they are never written by committees, and they stay with you. A great creed shares these traits.

Growing up Catholic, I was obliged to recite the Apostles' Creed: *I believe in God, the Father almighty, creator of heaven and earth.* There were twelve points of belief, and they have remained in my head. They have fuelled religious belief for hundreds of years. It is a creed that has outlasted empires.

Essentially a creed is a statement of beliefs, and it is the foundation for any business. *What do you believe?* This question is the critical starting point for acquiring passion capital. It's a simple question. But the answer isn't always simple.

A creed comes from our personal experience, from our successes and failures, from mentors and family, from faith, challenges, and loss. It comes out of both disappointment and hope. A good creed creates unity, clarity, and inspiration.

I Believe

Years ago, on one of my first trips to New York, I found myself at Rockefeller Plaza, and I noticed the plaque that has John D. Rockefeller Jr.'s family creed written on it. Titled "I Believe," it says, "I believe that every right implies a responsibility; every opportunity, an obligation; every possession, a duty." Rockefeller's father, John Sr., had a lot of possessions. By the beginning of the twentieth century he had become America's first billionaire, and the richest man in the world (*Forbes* estimated his net worth in 2007 dollars to be $663.4 billion, which would make him roughly twelve times richer than Bill Gates). The last entry on Rockefeller's list of beliefs is, "I believe that love is the greatest thing in the world; that it alone can overcome hate; that right can and will triumph over might."

Rockefeller Sr. wasn't above using (economic) might to triumph over right. He bought out his competitors, and if they refused to sell he told them he'd drive them into bankruptcy, then buy up their assets at auction. According to the *New York World* newspaper, Rockefeller's company, Standard Oil, was "the most cruel, impudent, pitiless, and grasping monopoly ever fastened upon a country."

So he had his detractors. But Rockefeller was also the father of modern philanthropy, giving billions to charity, and reshaping the nature of charity itself. Even when he was making fifty cents a day as an assistant bookkeeper, he was giving part of his salary to charity. He devoted the last forty years of his life to philanthropy, and during those years he financed the University of Chicago and Spelman College, a college in Atlanta for African-American women. In 1913, he donated $250 million (roughly $5 billion in today's dollars) to create the Rockefeller Foundation, of which John Jr. was the first president. It was America's first global foundation and became a key contributor to education, public health (its first contribution was to the American Red Cross), science, and the arts.

But what the foundation was really funding was innovation. Its reach was global, and it contributed to literacy in China, to agricultural innovation in Mexico, to racial equality in America. It also played a part in the development of the centrifuge, the electron microscope, and the computer. When a young Albert Einstein applied for $500, Rockefeller said, "Let's give him $1,000. He may be onto something."

Rockefeller's creed has stayed with me. His foundation has disbursed more than $14 billion since its inception and is still going strong, guided by that creed. Rockefeller was of another time, but his extraordinary charitable efforts showed him to be a passion capitalist.

The Rockefeller Creed

I believe in the supreme worth of the individual and in his right to life, liberty and the pursuit of happiness;

I believe that every right implies a responsibility; every opportunity, an obligation; every possession, a duty;

I believe that the law was made for man and not man for the law; that government is the servant of the people and not their master;

I believe in the dignity of labour, whether with head or hand; that the world owes no man a living but that it owes every man an opportunity to make a living;

I believe that thrift is essential to well-ordered living and that economy is a prime requisite of a sound financial structure, whether in government, business or personal affairs;

I believe that truth and justice are fundamental to an enduring social order;

I believe in the sacredness of a promise, that a man's word should be as good as his bond; that his character – not wealth or power or position – is of supreme worth;

I believe that the rendering of useful service is the common duty of mankind and that only in the purifying fire of sacrifice is the dross of selfishness consumed and the greatness of the human soul set free;

I believe in an all-wise and all-loving God, named by whatever name, and that the individual's highest fulfillment, greatest happiness and widest usefulness are to be found in living in harmony with His will;

I believe that love is the greatest thing in the world; that it alone can overcome hate; that right can and will triumph over might.

Heart versus Marketing

The idea of what a creed is has been degraded in recent years. You can go into any business and see a "mission statement" or a "vision statement" posted at the reception or on a wall somewhere. Sometimes it's a legitimate expression of a company's character and aims. More often, it is a marketing vehicle, put together by a team looking to make a good impression. Sometimes such statements are glib – "The Customer is King." Occasionally they are religious in tone. They can be afterthoughts, or PR exercises, or damage control.

But an authentic and well-crafted statement of belief can be a powerful tool.

In 2010, I was in the Toronto offices of Johnson & Johnson. The company's credo was posted in the reception area, and I stood there and read it. It was written in 1943 by Gen. Robert Wood Johnson. He saw the credo as both a moral code and a blueprint for business success. It begins, "We believe our first responsibility is to the doctors, nurses and patients, to mothers and fathers and all others who use our products and services." The J&J credo thus outlines a hierarchy: starting with doctors and nurses and customers, and moving down to employees – "They must have a sense of security in their jobs. Compensation must be fair and adequate . . . employees must feel free to make suggestions and complaints." What was most interesting to me was farther down, in the last paragraph: "Our final responsibility is to our stockholders."

If you've been listening to CEOs being interviewed in the last few years, you might find many of them declaring that their *first* responsibility is to the stockholder. It could be a creed for hundreds of companies these days – "The Stockholder is King." The problem with having kings for stockholders is that it reduces the worth of the company to the performance of its last quarter. Miss your projections and the kings say, "Off with your head!"

Over the years, J&J stockholders have made a great deal of money, but that is because the stockholder *isn't* king. He is important, but it isn't the quarterly pressure on the share price that determines what decisions are made. It is the commitment to quality and innovation and responsibility. And those beliefs that General Johnson laid out in 1943 have been severely tested.

In 1982, seven people died after taking cyanide-laced capsules of Extra-Strength Tylenol, which at the time was J&J's bestselling product, accounting for 17 per cent of its net income. The tampering had occurred after the bottles left J&J, but the company assumed responsibility for dealing with the situation. They immediately recalled 31 million bottles of Tylenol and offered free replacements. In what is sometimes labelled "the recall that started them all," J&J put their customers' safety first. The recall and relaunch of Tylenol cost Johnson & Johnson $100 million. At the time, a lot of people felt the brand would never recover, that the company itself might not recover. Yet both not only survived but flourished. Consumers and investors alike admired the swift and forthright way the company dealt with the crisis, the way it put public health ahead of short-term profit.

The stock took a hit initially but quickly recovered. A $1,000 investment in the company in 1982 would be worth $26,400 now, not including their generous dividend, which increased for forty-nine consecutive years. Johnson & Johnson has emerged as one of the most successful companies in America.

Stock prices are transitory but principles are lasting.

At the heart of J&J's success is the creed written in 1943. The company has weathered other storms, and each time it has acted according to its creed. In 2010, J&J recalled two hip-replacement products after finding that one in eight recipients needed revision surgery within five years. In 2011, there were several recalls, among them another recall of certain Tylenol and Benadryl products. They also recalled 360,000 units of a product used to drain surgical wounds. In each instance, they quickly and voluntarily recalled the defective product.

When I asked the J&J receptionist what the credo meant to her, she went on enthusiastically. It's posted everywhere, she told me, and all employees had to learn it. She said it governed her actions and attitudes. I got a similar response from the executive assistant to the president, and from the president himself.

In other words, it's effective. All of the company's decisions stemmed from that credo. None of the decisions were easy ones to take. They all threatened the immediate bottom line, and certain investors were nervous. But Johnson & Johnson stayed the course, proving their critics wrong. It is a good model for aspiring passion capitalists. Don't be swayed by outside forces if you're convinced that what you are doing is the right thing.

The creed posted in the reception area of Johnson & Johnson's offices read as follows:

Our Credo

We believe our first responsibility is to the doctors, nurses and patients, to mothers and fathers and all others who use our products and services.

In meeting their needs everything we do must be of high quality.

We must constantly strive to reduce our costs in order to maintain reasonable prices.

Customers' orders must be serviced promptly and accurately.

Our supplier and distributors must have an opportunity to make a fair profit.

We are responsible to our employees, the men and women who work with us throughout the world.

Everyone must be considered as an individual.

We must respect their dignity and recognize their merit.

They must have a sense of security in their jobs.

Compensation must be fair and accurate, and working conditions clean, orderly and safe.

We must be mindful of ways to help our employees fulfill their family responsibilities.

Employees must feel free to make suggestions and complaints.

There must be equal opportunity for employment, development and advancement for those qualified.

We must provide competent management, and their actions must be just and ethical.

We are responsible to the communities in which we live and work and to the world community as well.

We must be good citizens – support good works and charities and bear our fair share of taxes.

We must encourage civic improvements and better health and education.

We must maintain in good order the property we are privileged to use, protecting the environment and natural resources.

Our final responsibility is to our stockholders.

Business must make a sound profit.

We must experiment with new ideas.

Research must be carried on, innovative programs developed and mistakes paid for.

New equipment must be purchased, new facilities provided and new products launched.

Reserves must be created to provide for adverse times.

When we operate according to these principles, the stockholders should realize a fair return.

The Evolution of a Creed

Creeds don't need to remain the same in order to be effective. On the contrary, sometimes they need to evolve to address a changing environment. Company leaders need to take a hard look at what the company was when it began and what it has become and make necessary adjustments. Part of being a great leader is understanding when to reassess a course of action and when to stay the course. The Ford Motor Company is a great example.

Henry Ford wasn't a revolutionary carmaker. Fiat beat him to the market. Others built more interesting cars. What Ford did was democratize the automobile. His original creed began with the line, "I will build a motor car for the great multitude."

He did. The Model T was a homely sedan that began production in 1908 and came in one colour – black – and wasn't known for its performance or for technological innovation. The innovation came in the way it was manufactured. Ford built an assembly line that produced thousands of them, which brought costs down, which made the cars affordable.

"It will be so low in price that no man making a good salary will be unable to own one – and enjoy with his family the blessing of hours of pleasure in God's great open spaces."

The Model T stopped production in 1927. Eighty years later there were fewer of God's great open spaces and a lot more competition. Ford Motors had become complacent. It had ceased to innovate, and it failed to see where the market was heading. The world wanted more economical cars. People were less enthusiastic about SUVs; they wanted economy and affordability. They wanted, in effect, a modern version of the Model T. There were new versions out there; unfortunately for Ford, most of them were being manufactured by the Japanese and the Koreans.

In 1997, Ford's share of the American market was still a healthy 25 per cent. Nine years later it was 14 per cent, and that year the company posted a loss of $12.7 billion. It had fallen behind Toyota. For the first time, the Big Three car manufacturers weren't exclusively American.

In September 2006, Alan R. Mulally was named president and CEO of Ford. An outsider to the auto industry, he was given the task of turning around Ford's declining sales, slumping profits, and loss of market share. In February 2007, Mulally addressed a meeting of a hundred Ford staff members and bluntly told them, "We have been going out of business for forty years."

A new creed was written. It doesn't sit behind the receptionist's desk at head office. It wasn't posted as an inspirational tool on the walls of Ford dealerships. It was a creed that was circulated only among management, and it honestly and concisely reflected how far the company had fallen and how they were going to climb out of that hole.

In 2010, Ford showed a profit of $6.6 billion, the largest in a decade. And this even though it was the only one of the original Big Three that didn't accept a government bailout. Employee profit-sharing bonuses were distributed. Ford was back on track. Their post-recession success started with a clear and honest statement of beliefs. It started with a new creed, one that offered a harsh assessment of where they were, re-examined the company culture and its failings, and determined what they could accomplish.

The Princess Margaret Experience

My mother's death from cancer was a life-changing experience for me. Watching someone you love die a slow, painful death is devastating, but it became a source of inspiration as well. In September 2003, I became president and CEO of the Princess Margaret Hospital Foundation, which supports the Princess Margaret cancer centre in Toronto.

My first challenge was to define and focus our beliefs. You might think our goal was obvious: to conquer cancer. But cancer is a complex disease, and after canvassing surgeons, radiation oncologists, and medical oncologists, I discovered they all had their own set of beliefs on how to approach the problem. Basic researchers, translational researchers, and clinical researchers did as well. Not to mention patients, volunteers, and management.

Having defined our beliefs, how could we work all of these beliefs into a concise creed? We needed to come up with something that would unify rather than divide – a statement that would bring clarity, that possessed both honesty and hope.

On our board was Chris Jordan, president of Young & Rubicam, Toronto, part of the international marketing and communications agency. Y&R had developed creed statements for several of their clients, and I was moved by how authentic and powerful those statements were. I asked them to craft one for us.

One key to creating effective creed statements is to get a lot of input but have only one writer. It took a year to gather all the necessary information from all interested parties and collate and digest it. When we had everything in place, we had Joe Hash of Y&R write it. He wrote from the heart, and Y&R did this pro bono. This is what he delivered.

Conquer Cancer In Our Lifetime

It may seem like we've been fighting this fight forever. But we haven't.

There was a time, not long ago, when cancer was a death sentence. And the treatment was dreaded almost as much as the disease. We've seen that change in our lifetime, at the Princess Margaret.

We've seen the entire process of cancer care forever altered. We've seen radical mastectomies become lumpectomies. We've seen the precision of image-guided therapies spare more healthy tissue. We've seen undreamed-of advances at the cellular level and revolutionary work in healing beyond the body.

All in our lifetime. All at the Princess Margaret.

We see the things we do give hope to millions, one

person at a time. We've transformed a provincial cancer hospital into one of the world's top five cancer research centres. As a proud partner of the University Health Network, we've grown our people into the thousands. We see leading researchers, from all over the world, leave their home to come here. Because this is where they believe the fight will be finished. In our lifetime.

Yes, we are still losing people to cancer. But more and more, we are controlling the cancer, instead of the cancer controlling us. We now know that every cancer is as individual as the patient. So we're developing personalized care that delivers the right treatment to the right patient at the right time. This is the future of cancer medicine, and we are on the forefront of that progress today.

It may seem like we'll be fighting this fight forever. But we won't. Because we're closing in. We have the momentum. We have the talent. And we have the passion. This is the front line. We are Canada's cancer warriors. But we can't do it alone.

The world needs to hear the Princess Margaret message. So share it at every opportunity with anyone who will listen.

It's a simple message, really. But it's a message of incredible power: we are conquering cancer at Canada's cancer research centre, the Princess Margaret. In our lifetime.

I read this out loud to eighty people at the Princess Margaret – senior research staff, oncologists, clinicians, and senior hospital leadership, a group that was diverse in background, training, vision, and work culture. At the end of it they all applauded. We had found our creed.

Finding Your Creed: What Do You Believe?

The first step in creating a creed is to get rid of any generic creed you or your company may have inherited, anything inauthentic that says, "we will exceed our customers' expectations" or "we will be a recognized leader" or "people are our most important asset."

Jargon has replaced belief in the corporate world, to our detriment. Vision statements that were put together by committees tend to be sanitized, lifeless, and unfocused. Sometimes they're dishonest. An authentic creed may make some people uncomfortable. It's supposed to.

You probably have a personal creed – what you believe and what you believe in. You probably don't have it written down, but doing so is a useful place to start. What do you feel passionate about? What are the beach ball questions you can't hold down, that nag at you? You may fervently believe the Maple Leafs are going to win the Stanley Cup, but you need to go deeper than that. That isn't enough to build a creed on (although thousands of diehard fans have certainly tried). Articulating your beliefs, getting them down in writing, is a starting point.

Developing a statement for your company involves a bit more research. Here are seven steps for creating a company creed:

1. DO BACKGROUND RESEARCH

Start by reading whatever strategy documents already exist. Look at market research, press reports, and industry-related material. Make sure you have a firm grasp of the company's history, its people, accomplishments, failures, stories, and aspirations. It's difficult not to have assumptions about any company, but it's important to put them aside and look at the data.

2. INTERVIEW LEADERSHIP

Sit down with management and talk to them about what their own goals and beliefs are. What are their dreams? What does success look like to them? Note where their emotions and their commitments intersect. Not everyone sees a company the same way. You need to get a sense of the different perspectives in order to find common ground.

3. HOLD FOCUS GROUPS

The focus group has gotten a bad rap in some quarters these days, but it can be a valuable tool. At the Princess Margaret we had focus groups with patients, volunteers, supporters, and staff. We were looking to find out what worked and what didn't, about our strengths and weaknesses in our service, about outcomes versus expectations. We heard personal stories – some that were tragic, others that were inspirational. Most critical to our creed were stories that invoked passion, pain, humour, and loss.

4. WRITE A BRIEFING DOCUMENT

The next step is to gather all this feedback into a briefing document. You need to be able to effectively summarize not just the stories but the energy and passion behind them. You need a clear sense of how many different viewpoints are out there and where the intersections lie. The briefing document should be structured around the most important questions, using the actual words of those who answered the questions, in a way that provides a useful narrative.

5. WRITE YOUR CREED

The key here is to have only one writer. A committee will probably dilute the briefing document rather than focus it. This critical step requires focus; the creed has to be written with clarity and honesty. The first draft must be powerful, on-target, and authentic. It should be based on real stories, real challenges, and real progress.

6. BUILD SUPPORT

I tried out Princess Margaret's creed by reading it out loud to different groups at the hospital – leaders, volunteers, community supporters. I started with small groups and asked for their reaction rather than their feedback. (It's a fine distinction, I know.) My feeling was that this creed was working. If the creed works, then stick with it. The committee approach can still kill the creed's essential passion at this point. Don't be blind to criticism, but don't let the creed get pecked to death, either. It's a good idea to be pretty sure the creed works before presenting a final version.

7. INTEGRATE THE CREED

The final step is to integrate the creed into the culture, using it in strategy, planning, communication, branding, government, media relations, and fundraising. The Princess Margaret Hospital Foundation creed gave us a unified message to take to the world. But it did more than that: it unified *us*. That is the strength of an effective creed.

A creed can be used to define a career, a company, a cause, or even a country. It is the essential foundation of passion capital. Without a creed, the other principles don't work. Passion capital can't exist without a strong foundation.

KEY LESSONS

1. A creed is a focused statement of beliefs that creates clarity, unity, and inspiration. Creed is the DNA of passion capital.

2. The inspiration for a creed comes from personal experiences, from successes and failures, from mentors and family, from community, faith, ambition, and passion.

3. A creed articulates beliefs and priorities; it answers the question: "What do we believe?"

4. Developing a creed is the first and most important building block of passion capital.

3

CULTURE:

GROWING YOUR BELIEFS

*Culture is the process by which a person becomes
all that they were created capable of being.*
THOMAS CARLYLE

Several years ago I was in the Thomson Building, in
Toronto, to meet with Geoffrey Beattie, who is the
president of the Woodbridge Company, the holding company
for the Thomsons, Canada's wealthiest family. I went down
the hall to the small kitchen to get myself a cup of coffee. Ken
Thomson was there, making himself some instant soup. At
the time, he was the ninth-richest man in the world, worth
approximately $19.6 billion. Enough, certainly, to afford a
nice lunch. I looked at the soup he was stirring. "It suits me
just fine," he said, smiling.

Thomson understood value. Neighbours reported seeing
him leave his local grocery store with jumbo packages of tis-
sues that were on sale. He bought off-the-rack suits and had
his old shoes resoled. Yet he had no difficulty paying almost

$76 million for a painting (for Peter Paul Rubens's *Massacre of the Innocents*, in 2002, the most expensive Old Master work sold at auction at the time). He sought value, whether it was in business, art, or groceries.

In 1976, Thomson inherited a $500-million business empire that was built on newspapers, publishing, travel agencies, and oil. By the time he died, in 2006, his empire had grown to $25 billion.

He left both a financial legacy and an art legacy (many of the works he bought are hanging in the Art Gallery of Ontario), but his most lasting legacy might be the culture he created. Geoffrey Beattie, who worked closely with him, said that Ken wasn't a business genius. His success came from being a principled investor and from surrounding himself with good people and staying loyal to them. In return he earned their loyalty.

Thomson streamlined the family business, getting out of oil and out of the travel business before it was gutted by the Internet. He concentrated on a narrow range of investments in order to stay focused. "Don't water the wine," he used to say.

Thomson was always looking to the future – what would happen ten years from now? Fifty years from now? To see a business in the long term, you first have to define what your business is. Was he selling newspapers? Textbooks? The answer to both of these questions was yes, but what he was actually selling was information and knowledge. Understanding this, he got into digital publishing early on, especially for the legal and medical arms of his publishing empire. It gave him a jump on competitors. He also sold off the Thomson textbook division, divesting himself of an asset that was being eroded by digital publishing. He understood that we would always need information, but we wouldn't necessarily be getting it in the same way we had for the last several centuries.

For the long-term viability of any enterprise, Thomson understood that you needed a viable corporate culture. It, too, had to be long-term. So he cultivated good people and kept them. Thomson worked with honest and competent business managers and gave them his long-term commitment and support. From these modest principles, an empire grew.

Thomson created a culture that extended out from him and has lived after him. The passion capitalist passes on, but the passion capital remains in the form of the empire he left and the culture that pervades it.

Fertile Soil

Once a creed has been successfully created, once your beliefs have been laid out, the next step is to create an environment where they can grow. You need a culture that allows your beliefs to bloom. You need fertile soil. How do you find that?

Here are eight rules for creating the right conditions for a culture that reflects your creed:

1. HIRE THE RIGHT PEOPLE

Hire for passion and commitment first, experience second, and credentials third. There is no shortage of impressive CVs out there, but you should try to find people who are interested in the same things you are. You don't want to be simply a stepping stone on an employee's journey toward his or her own (very different) passion. Asking the right questions is key: What do you love about your chosen career? What inspires you? What courses in school did you dread? You want to get a sense of what the potential employee believes.

2. COMMUNICATE

Once you have the right people, you need to sit down regularly with them and discuss what is going well and what isn't. It's critical to take note of your victories, but it's just as important to analyze your losses. A fertile culture is one that recognizes when things don't work and adjusts to rectify the problem. As well, people need to feel safe and trusted, to understand that they can speak freely without fear of repercussion.

The art of communication tends to put the stress on talking, but listening is equally important. Great cultures grow around people who listen, not just to each other or to their clients and stakeholders. It's also important to listen to what's happening outside your walls. What is the market saying? What is the current zeitgeist? What developments, trends, and calamities are going on?

3. TEND TO THE WEEDS

A culture of passion capital can be compromised by the wrong people. One of the most destructive corporate weeds is the whiner. Whiners aren't necessarily public with their complaints. They don't stand up in meetings and articulate everything they think is wrong with the company. Instead, they move through the organization, speaking privately, sowing doubt, strangling passion. Sometimes this is simply the nature of the beast: they whined at their last job and will whine at the next. Sometimes these people simply aren't a good fit. Your passion isn't theirs. Constructive criticism is healthy, but relentless complaining is toxic. Identify these people and replace them.

4. WORK HARD, PLAY HARD

To obtain passion capital requires a work ethic. It's easy to do what you love. In the global economy we can measure who has a superior work ethic, who is leading in productivity. Not many industries these days thrive on a forty-hour work week. A culture where everyone understands that long hours are sometimes required will work if this sacrifice is recognized and rewarded.

5. BE AMBITIOUS

"Make no little plans: they have no magic to stir men's blood." These words were uttered by Daniel Burnham, the Chicago architect whose vision recreated the city after the great fire of 1871. The result of his ambition is an extraordinary American city that still has the magic to stir men's blood. Ambition is sometimes seen as a negative these days, but without it we would stagnate. You need a culture that supports big steps and powerful beliefs.

You can see these qualities in cities that have transformed themselves. Cities are the most visible examples of successful and failed cultures. Bilbao and Barcelona did so and became the envy of the world and prime tourist destinations. Pittsburgh reinvented itself when the steel industry withered. But Detroit wasn't able to do the same when the auto industry took a dive.

6. CELEBRATE DIFFERENCES

When choosing students for a program, most universities consider more than just marks. If you had a dozen straight-A students who were from the same socio-economic background and the same geographical area, you might not get much in the way of interesting debate or interaction. Great cultures are built on a diversity of background, experience, and interests. These differences generate energy, which is critical to any enterprise.

7. CREATE THE SPACE

Years ago, scientists working in laboratories were often in underground bunkers and rarely saw their colleagues; secrecy was prized. Now innovation is prized. In cutting-edge research and academic buildings, architects try to promote as much interaction as possible. They design spaces where people from different disciplines will come together, whether in workspace or in common leisure space. Their reasoning is simple: it is this interaction that helps breed revolutionary ideas. Creative and Engineering chat over coffee. HR and Marketing bump into one another in the fitness centre. Culture is made in the physical space. Look at your space and ask, "Does it promote interaction and connectivity?"

8. TAKE THE LONG VIEW

If your culture is dependent on this quarter's earnings or this month's sales targets, then it is handicapped by short-term thinking. Passion capitalists take the long view. We tend to overestimate what we can do in a year, but underestimate what we can do in five years. The culture needs to look ahead, not just in months but in years and even decades.

The writer Arthur Koestler said that a writer's ambition should be to trade a hundred contemporary readers for ten readers in ten years' time and for one reader in a hundred years' time. Lasting influence is better than a burst of fame. Keep an eye on the long view.

Do Unto Others

Isadore Sharp built his Four Seasons Hotels and Resorts chain on a simple premise, the golden rule: treat others as you would like to be treated. This may seem an obvious creed for someone in the hospitality industry. But Sharp's creed extends to his employees. A lot of hotel work isn't glamorous. You make beds, clean rooms, clear tables in the restaurants. Sharp understood that to have happy customers, he needed happy employees. Part of his philosophy was to put employees first, and to give them the flexibility and authority to help clients.

Whenever possible, he hires local talent and promotes from within. To help keep his eye on the future, he signs management to long-term contracts. He hires for personality and then trains for technical skills. You can teach people how to run the front desk or make a bed, but you can't teach passion.

Four Seasons hotels are synonymous with luxury. The hotels are beautiful, the rooms are great. But the true essence of luxury is in the experience. And people are more critical than furniture when it comes to the experience. As Sharp has said, it isn't the complaint the customer remembers, but the outcome. That's why his employees are empowered to make decisions on the spot. "We have to have employees who think for themselves and act on it," he has said.

By empowering those employees, Sharp was essentially giving them a greater stake in the company. He was also communicating the idea that they were both important and trusted. "I was saying that people who had been considered expendable by management now had to come first." It is a good recipe for loyalty.

Sharp's philosophy has resulted in one of the most successful corporate cultures in the world.

The Princess Margaret Culture

When I started hiring people for the Princess Margaret Hospital Foundation, the first thing I looked for was passion. People who have fought cancer themselves, or who have watched a loved one in that fight, tend to have an indefatigable desire to defeat cancer. Sadly, this is still a large group.

When you read obituaries, you inevitably come across the phrase, "after a brave battle with cancer." It is indeed a battlefield. And we are dedicated to winning the battle. To do that, we needed a culture that was stable and thriving; one that was built for the future.

There is a finite pool of money to draw on, and we understood that we needed a culture of innovation to raise the kind of money necessary to fund our research. We built brands and created intellectual property to raise money for the hospital, but we also licensed these out to other organizations, both national and global, to advance their cancer programs. Our Ride to Conquer Cancer raised $16 million. We subsequently loaned the program to cancer organizations in Vancouver, Calgary, and Montreal. It has been recognized as one of the world's most successful cycling fundraising events.

We were also able to secure the largest private donation to cancer research in the history of Canada, as a result of our close and trusted relationship with the Campbell family, part of the Thomson clan. We have a created a culture that drives critical science and medicine, and in the process we have become one of the top five cancer research centres in the world. We are "Canada's Cancer Warriors."

In 2010, the Princess Margaret Hospital Foundation was proud to receive a Canada's 10 Most Admired Corporate Cultures award from Waterstone Human Capital. Ours was a culture that we nurtured carefully, one that is based on our creed ("We are Canada's cancer warriors").

Camelot and the Culture of Possibility

Few political cultures were as potent and mythologized as John F. Kennedy's brief time in office. He embodied an era.

We look back on it as a time of prosperity, but we sometimes forget the nuclear tensions that gripped the world then, the issues that divided us. We think of Kennedy as the most popular president, but we forget he was elected by the slimmest margin in presidential history at the time (115,000 votes). Nevertheless, in his short tenure Kennedy profoundly shaped America's political culture and the country itself.

His inaugural address was short (the fourth shortest among presidents, at just under fourteen minutes), but it is still remembered as one of the best. The line that most people remember is, "Ask not what your country can do for you – ask what you can do for your country." This brief speech was Kennedy's creed, and with it he established a number of key points. He made a plea for everyone to pull together, to work to make the country great. But he also offered an unusual (for politics) timeline: "All this will not be finished in the first hundred days. Nor will it be finished in the first thousand days, nor in the life of this Administration, nor even perhaps in our lifetime on this planet. But let us begin."

Kennedy himself communicated a new start. He was young and charismatic, two qualities that weren't seen in his opponent Richard Nixon, nor in former presidents Dwight Eisenhower and Harry Truman. He talked about the future. He *looked* like the future. He communicated the sense that the country was at the beginning of a bold era of sacrifice and accomplishment. He created a culture based on that creed, a culture that formed quickly and was infused with both hope and purpose. "Let the word go forth," he said in that inaugural address, "that the torch has been passed to a new generation of Americans."

Kennedy communicated a lot in a few words. The culture that formed around him and his creed was one of possibility. It was Kennedy's administration that founded the Peace Corps. Its goal was to promote world peace and friendship and to provide technical assistance to emerging countries. Kennedy also saw it as a way of countering the image of "the ugly American" that was entrenched abroad. Since 1961 more than two hundred thousand Americans have served in the Peace Corps.

Kennedy also tabled the Civil Rights Act, which outlawed segregation and also outlawed discrimination against women and African-Americans. The Civil Rights Act wasn't a unifying piece of legislation. Kennedy knew this, but he also knew it was a necessary step to keep the country great. He was prepared to make an unpopular decision for long-term benefits.

Kennedy's passion capital ignited not just his own country but much of the world. Under Kennedy, America was admired and envied abroad. JFK and Jackie were celebrities in Europe and in Canada, where they were a bigger draw than the Queen.

The political comedian Bill Maher once commented on the way the United States was perceived in the early twenty-first century. "We used to be loved and admired around the world," he said. "Now we're the asshole. How did we become the asshole?"

A lot can happen to a culture in forty years.

Lessons from a Dead Culture

The downfall of the Easter Island society that erected those famous giant stone heads holds some lessons for us. Eight hundred years ago it was a successful, complex culture, one that had the leisure time, the technical ingenuity, and the artistic ability to make those iconic statues.

But clans on the island got caught up in a competition to build the largest and most dramatic statue. To move the giant blocks of stone, they had to cut down trees, which were trimmed and used to roll the tons of stone along to the coast, where they were erected.

Easter Island isn't large – it's just 64 square miles. Trees were cut down to facilitate what essentially became an arms race. There are 887 statues. Whole forests disappeared. At some point, there was a single tree left standing. What went through their minds at that point?

They cut it down. No one kept any seeds to grow more trees. The culture had dedicated itself to a single, artistically remarkable, but ultimately destructive cause. When the last tree was gone, there was no more wood to make fires. There was no wood to build boats. The birds that nested in the trees were gone, and the mice and rats and insects they had preyed upon were now without predators and flourished.

The culture collapsed. But it wasn't just the culture that collapsed. The entire ecosystem collapsed.

When a culture loses perspective on what is important, it is doomed. It happened on Easter Island five hundred years ago, where the only goal was scale: to build the biggest. Some of the standing heads are 33 feet high and weigh 86 tons. One of the last, unfinished heads, still lying on the ground, not yet erected, would have been 69 feet high. It weighed 270 tons. There is a grim lesson here.

A successful culture doesn't lose perspective. It doesn't pursue profit and expansion at the expense of all else. It shifts, it evolves, but it remains true to the creed that it is based on.

KEY LESSONS

1. Culture is the fertile soil where your beliefs take root and grow.

2. Successful cultures are built with a long-term commitment to performance and to basic human values like loyalty, respect, and passion.

3. Great cultures are based on clear, concrete principles such as the golden rule. Actions, not words, drive performance-based cultures.

4. A creed focuses and sustains culture.

4

COURAGE:

THE STRENGTH TO TAKE RISKS

Success is not final, failure is not fatal:
it is the courage to continue that counts.
WINSTON CHURCHILL

Courage is the third principle of passion capital. There are many definitions of courage. Hemingway called it "grace under pressure." Einstein thought it was the ability to go against the grain. "Any intelligent fool can make things bigger and more complex . . . ," he said. "It takes a touch of genius – and a lot of courage – to move in the opposite direction." Winston Churchill said "courage is what it takes to stand up and speak."

It is one thing to have a creed to live by, but it often takes courage to initiate that creed. A belief doesn't become a principle until it's tested, and that's why courage is a key component for passion capital.

In 2007, I was at a dinner in Toronto on the eve of the Toronto Marathon, which raises money for the Princess

Margaret Hospital, among other causes. The woman seated beside me was petite and pleasant. I asked her what she did. She said she was involved in setting up marathons. I nodded politely and we chatted. A few minutes later she got up and gave a PowerPoint presentation. What followed was a remarkable story of courage.

It turns out I'd been sitting next to Kathrine Switzer, the first woman to run the Boston Marathon. In 1967 Switzer was a nineteen-year-old journalism student at Syracuse University. At the time, women weren't allowed to run marathons, let alone the iconic Boston Marathon. And not even her track coach, Arnie Briggs, believed she could run the 26.2 miles. But he said if she proved she could do it, he'd take her to Boston.

Three weeks before the marathon, Switzer ran the distance for the first time. True to his word, Briggs entered her in the event, using her initial – K. Switzer. Her boyfriend, "Big Tom" Miller, a 235-pound former All American football player and nationally ranked hammer thrower, thought, "If she can run it, I can too." So he entered as well, as did Briggs.

It was snowing when the race started, and Switzer was in a grey hooded sweatshirt, like most of the runners on the course. Beneath the hood, though, she was wearing lipstick and earrings.

Around mile two, a press truck rolled by, a flatbed that had reporters and photographers on it. A man on the truck stared at her, pointed his finger, and screamed something. A few seconds later Switzer heard the sound of leather-soled shoes on the pavement coming up fast behind her; she knew it wasn't another runner. She turned and saw an angry face, teeth bared. It was Jock Semple, the race director. Semple was a big man and he grabbed her shoulder and screamed, "Get the hell out of my race and give me those numbers!" He tried to rip away the number that was pinned to the front of her sweatshirt. She was terrified and tried to run away. Semple grabbed the back of her sweatshirt.

There was a flash of orange as Big Tom Miller (wearing his Syracuse colours) threw a hard cross-body block into Semple, who landed on the roadside in a heap. Switzer's trainer, Arnie, yelled, "Run like hell!"

The journalists on the press truck told the driver to follow her. They knew where the story was. The truck caught up to her and reporters took photos and fired questions at her as she ran: "What are you trying to prove? When are you going to quit?"

The answer to the second question was: never.

Switzer finished the race, protected by Miller and other runners. She proved that a woman could run 26.2 miles. Seven years later she won the New York City Marathon.

Switzer devoted her life to setting up marathons for women in twenty-seven countries. The women's marathon was finally recognized as an official event in the 1984 Olympics, due in part to her lobbying. But it was that defining moment in 1967 that was the springboard for women's marathons. One woman had the courage to stand up (and run) for her beliefs. She could see that the only thing women lacked was opportunity. Kathrine Switzer had the courage of her beliefs.

My own definition of courage is having the strength to stand up for your beliefs. The more ground-breaking your belief, the more courage you need to stick with it. We saw it in Tiananmen Square, in Libya, in Egypt where people rose up against dictators.

And we see it in China today in Bo Xilai. Bo is a Chinese politician who isn't well known in the West. He doesn't fit the stereotype of Chinese politicians, who tend to be remote. Bo is tall and personable and accessible, Kennedyesque in demeanour. During Mao Zedong's Cultural Revolution, Bo spent five years in prison and another five in a hard-labour camp because his father was labelled a counter-revolutionary.

His subsequent political career has been marked by a war against the powerful crime organizations in Chongqing. Labelled Strike the Black, his campaign against organized crime resulted in five thousand arrests in eight months. He went after not just the gangsters but the corrupt politicians and police officials, including the deputy police commissioner, who had facilitated their criminal activities. Some of the people who were imprisoned were from his own administration. It takes courage to take on the bad guys. It takes even more courage when some of the bad guys are your colleagues. In a country where capitalism is just being defined, Bo is a passion capitalist, someone who has stood up for his beliefs despite the risks.

Fear of Failure

One of the standard definitions of courage is overcoming fear. Fear exists in individuals and companies and nations. What are we afraid of? We're afraid the decision we've just made will end our career. We're fearful of the competition, of our bosses, of the unknown, of the dark. We're afraid of failure.

Fear of failure, more than any other fear, prevents people from building passion capital. We are frozen into inactivity. We are afraid to move forward into unknown terrain. If you look at the biographies of successful people, there is often a pivotal moment when they made a decision that defined their career. Do I quit my engineering degree to found Research in Motion (Mike Lazaridis)? Do I bail out of the London School of Economics to start a rock band (Mick Jagger)?

Years ago there was an interesting commercial featuring Michael Jordan. As footage of his extraordinary athleticism played, his voice-over intoned, "I've missed more than nine thousand shots in my career. I've lost almost three hundred games. Twenty-six times I've been trusted to take the game-winning shot and missed." Recounting his failures only put his success in greater relief. In order to have the extraordinary success he did – Jordan was arguably the pre-eminent basketball player in history – he had to fail some of the time. A few of those failures probably still hurt. But his record remains one of the most remarkable in sport.

It is instructive to remember that while Babe Ruth led the American League in home runs for twelve seasons, he also led the league in strikeouts for five of those seasons. If you look at the list of all-time strikeout kings, you see the game's greatest hitters: Reggie Jackson (No. 1, with 2597 strikeouts), Sammy Sosa (No. 2 with 2306), José Canseco (No. 5 with 1942). It takes courage to keep swinging for the fences rather than playing it safe.

Accepting risk and being able to face our fear of failure is how we acquire courage. Failure is a part of greatness.

Betting the House

On September 16, 1992, a day that became known as "Black Wednesday," Hungarian-born businessman George Soros sold short more than $10 billion worth of English pounds. He was betting that the British government wouldn't raise its interest rates to levels that were comparable to those of other European Exchange Rate Mechanism countries, and that it wouldn't float its currency.

He was right. The U.K. withdrew from the European Exchange Rate Mechanism, devaluing the pound sterling. Soros made an estimated $1.1 billion in a day, and became known as "the man who broke the Bank of England."

Soros made his fortune as a speculator and investor. Speculating is, by definition, a high-risk activity. You don't always win. The key is to understand your failures. "I basically have survived by recognizing my mistakes," Soros has said.

Soros's interest in financial capital led to an interest in social capital. He has spent $7 billion on philanthropy. He gives his money away in the same spirit that he earned it. "His giving is openly political and daring," a colleague has said. "He is determined to change the nation's social agenda and is tough-minded about achieving his goals." He has financed a campaign to legalize marijuana for medicinal purposes, and spent millions trying to get George Bush Jr. defeated in the 2004 election. More than $1 billion went to efforts to democratize the Soviet bloc. He has funded immigrants' rights and education in the United States, and given to underprivileged children. Soros has called himself a failed philosopher. Philosophy's loss is philanthropy's gain. Having the courage to take risks can open up possibilities that we aren't always able to foresee.

Where do you find courage? In *The Wizard of Oz*, the Cowardly Lion thought the Wizard would give it to him. In the end, he found it within himself. No one can give it to you. You have to acquire it on your own.

Here are four ways to develop and utilize courage:

1. CALCULATE RISK

Passion capitalists have the courage to take risks. How do we define risk in this era? Banks were once synonymous with security. But they have failed, both literally (Bear Stearns, Lehman Brothers) and ethically. The expression "safe as houses" is now a cruel joke. Government bonds are no longer a safe haven, and not just the bonds of struggling countries like Greece and Ireland. Even the mighty U.S. was downgraded by Standard & Poor, going from a AAA rating to AA+, an unthinkable move only a few years ago.

The concept of risk has had to be redefined in recent years. Investors use probability analysis, game theory, technical analysis, and other increasingly complex tools to figure out where a stock is going.

Risk can be viewed in two ways. The first is to use logic and analysis: a single page of pros and cons, for example. The other is through instinct, what feels right in your gut. Risk analysis is best when both logic and instinct are used.

Regardless of what tools you are using, at some point you need courage to make a decision.

2. STAND BY YOUR BELIEFS

Would you stand in front of a column of tanks? As a prosecutor, would you take on the Mafia? Would you stand up to a government that could jail you indefinitely without trial?

We in the West live in mature (some would argue tired) democracies where almost half of citizens don't bother to vote. Apathy is an epidemic. One problem is that many people no longer have faith in our institutions or our governments, or even the capitalist system. Without strongly held beliefs, it's hard to sustain courage.

That's why creed is the first principle of passion capital. If our beliefs are resolute, we will find the courage to defend them.

3. LOVE IT OR LEAVE IT

It is difficult to be passionate about a job you hate. Some people spend their lives doing work they don't like. They started in a job they thought was temporary, something that would pay the rent, and planned to make the leap to what they dreamed of doing – going to law school, writing that novel, starting that tech company. What keeps them from actually doing it is a lack of courage. It's hard to make that leap. There are a dozen reasons not to – they have a mortgage, family, responsibilities; they need this paycheque. Though it's difficult to break away from our lives, it's even harder to spend a lifetime filled with regret.

4. FIND THE GREATER GOOD

Noble causes have always brought out courage in individuals. Every war is filled with stories of sacrifice and heroism. Self-interest guides human behaviour, but courage is often rooted in something larger than ourselves. When our beliefs are attached to a greater good, we often find a wellspring of courage.

The practices of team work are built around the concept of a greater good. You can assemble talented individuals who are unable to beat a team that is less talented but unified, one that is playing in the spirit of a greater good. We saw this in the 2004 Olympics, when the Americans sent a basketball team made up of superstar NBA players, including Tim Duncan, Allen Iverson, and young guns LeBron James and Carmelo Anthony. They were understandably cocky.

They lost their first game by a lopsided 19 points to lowly Puerto Rico. What happened? The Puerto Ricans were playing for something larger than themselves: the chance for their small country to beat the best in the world. They played as a team, and not only did they win, they dominated; it was the largest margin of defeat in U.S. international play. And Puerto Rico did it with a roster of unknowns.

In the medal round, the spectacular Americans lost to a unified and spirited Argentina team and had to settle for the bronze medal. It was a learning experience, though. At the next Olympics the Americans returned with a much more unified squad, one that felt the burden of national pride, one that possessed passion capital. In 2008 they claimed gold.

Courage in the Desert

"Political courage" is a phrase we rarely hear these days. Politics has less to do with principle than with polls. We need to look to history for an example.

One candidate is Golda Meir. She was born in Kiev, grew up in Milwaukee, and in 1969 became the first female prime minister of Israel (and the third female PM in modern history). She was an emotional presence during what were emotional times. Detractors accused her of leading with her heart and not her head. "It's no accident that many accuse me of conducting public affairs with my heart instead of my head," she once said. "Well, what if I do? Those who don't know how to weep with their whole heart don't know how to laugh either."

In 1948, Israel embarked on a fundraising drive in the United States. The treasurer of the Jewish Agency thought they might be able to raise $8 million. Meir went to America and managed to raise $50 million. David Ben-Gurion said it was Meir who found the money to make the Jewish state possible. Meir was one of the twenty-four signatories of the Jewish Declaration of Independence.

When she was elected prime minister in 1969 she had already been living with lymphoma for several years. Her political courage was matched by her personal courage.

In 1973, when Syrian forces were gathering on the Golan Heights, preparing for the Yom Kippur War, Meir decided not to launch a pre-emptive attack. She reasoned (correctly) that if it appeared that Israel had initiated the war, the United States wouldn't deliver the foreign aid and weapons Israel needed. It was an unpopular decision that took courage, but it was borne out when U.S. Secretary of State Henry Kissinger later confirmed that the United States wouldn't have sent Israel anything if it was seen as the aggressor. Sometimes what you don't do takes more courage than what you do.

Israel's very existence was an act of courage. The state was isolated, surrounded by enemies. Meir was there at its inception and she guided it through some of its most difficult trials. She personified the courage of the state.

You Can't Always Get What You Want

Toronto music impresario Michael Cohl promoted his first concert in 1969. Cohl had dropped out of York University and desperately wanted to be a rock promoter, but the band managers weren't returning his calls. He finally called country singer Buck Owens's manager, who did return Cohl's call. It wasn't rock and roll but it was a start. Cohl booked Owens and the cast of the television show *Hee Haw* into Maple Leaf Gardens, the cavernous hockey arena. The popular, if corny, country hoedown show was a big draw in many markets. But urban Toronto, it turned out, wasn't one of them; Cohl sold 2300 tickets for the 18,000-seat facility. When Owens looked out at the sparse crowd, he demanded the balance of his fee. Without a cheque for $25,000, he told Cohl, he wasn't going on. The crowd, such as it was, was getting restless.

Cohl didn't have the money. He went upstairs to the apartment of Harold Ballard, the eccentric owner of both the arena and the Maple Leafs hockey team, and asked if he could borrow $25,000. Surprisingly, Ballard wrote a cheque. Cohl took it downstairs to Owens, who put it in his pocket, then quickly played his hits.

Cohl's next show, with Ravi Shankar, lost money too. His third outing was also a failure, but at least it was a rock show, more or less (Melanie, Poco). His early efforts weren't successful, but they provided valuable lessons. He finally made money with a show that combined Rare Earth and Johnny Winter at Maple Leaf Gardens (and was able to pay Ballard back, eventually forming a partnership with Ballard's son).

It wasn't until 1988 that Michael Cohl changed the face of the concert business. That year he'd heard rumours that the Rolling Stones were going to tour. They hadn't toured in seven years, and by the day's rock standards, they were considered to be getting long in the tooth. Could they still draw?

Cohl thought they could, and he wanted to manage their tour. Cohl knew Steve O'Rourke, the manager of Pink Floyd, who in turn knew the grandly named Prince Rupert Lowenstein, the manager for the Rolling Stones. Through O'Rourke, Cohl got a meeting with Lowenstein, who arranged a meeting with the Stones.

Cohl had the idea of essentially buying the tour. He would guarantee the Stones a substantial figure up front (reputed to be $65 million, a stratospheric number for the time) in return for most of the rights (such as tickets and merchandising). Cohl flew down to the Caribbean and made the pitch to Mick Jagger and Lowenstein. The legendary promoter Bill Graham, who had managed the Stones' last tour and who was, at the time, the undisputed P. T. Barnum of rock, had just made his own pitch only minutes earlier. Cohl went in with his revolutionary offer. The next day the Stones signed a deal with Cohl. On the flight back to Toronto, Cohl turned to his business partner Norman Perry and said, "Oh Christ, it's over, we're bankrupt. This is the stupidest thing any human on earth would ever do."

The Steel Wheels/Urban Jungle tour, as it was billed, grossed almost $100 million in ticket sales in North America alone. Merchandise accounted for another $50 million. That tour became a blueprint for the way rock tours would be managed in the future. Cohl did a Pink Floyd tour in 1993 that surpassed the Stones' gross, then did another Stones tour that surpassed that. He went on to do four more Stones tours, as well as U2 and the Who, before turning his attention to Broadway musicals.

Cohl's belief that an aging band could still draw, that he could reinvent the rock tour and make it more profitable than a band's record sales, was both revolutionary and counter-intuitive. The decision to put up $65 million in support of that belief took courage.

Cohl is a passion capitalist because he took a risk to achieve something he believed in. And like so many other passion capitalists, he used his expertise and connections in the service of a cause. It was Cohl who put on the SARS benefit concert in Toronto, one of the largest rock events ever staged. Half a million people gathered at a decommissioned military base in north Toronto to hear AC/DC, Rush, and a dozen other acts. The headliners were the Rolling Stones, who played for free. The concert showed the world that Toronto, which was under a health advisory from the World Health

Organization at the time and was losing tourism dollars, was safe and thriving.

The writer Maya Angelou wrote that courage was the most important of all the virtues because without it we can't practise any other virtue with consistency. We can't be kind, true, merciful, generous, or honest. "One isn't necessarily born with courage," she wrote, "but one is born with potential."

Our challenge is to realize that potential.

KEY LESSONS

1.   Courage is having the strength to stand up for your beliefs and to take risks. Courage is the soul of passion capital.

2.   Courage flows from a strong creed and gives us the means to overcome our fear of failure.

3.   Fear of failure prevents us from building passion capital. If you hit the bull's eye every time, you are standing much too close to the target.

4.   No one can give you courage. You must find and develop it on your own. Courage is born out of adversity, challenge, and making mistakes.

5.   Transformational change always requires courage.

5

BRAND:

YOUR PROMISE TO THE WORLD

A brand for a company is like a reputation for a person.
You earn reputation by trying to do hard things well.
JEFF BEZOS

In 1997, I moved to California to work as the general manager and executive vice-president for the Disney Store. My job was to oversee five hundred North American Disney Stores and the fifteen thousand employees who worked in them. Along with seventeen other senior executives, I flew in the company jet to Walt Disney World in Orlando to take part in Disney Dimensions, an executive training course. As part of the exercise we were obliged to dress up as Disney characters and circulate in the park. I was dressed as the Sheriff of Nottingham. I walked around in the Florida humidity smiling and waving. Two little girls ran away from me crying. My colleagues were dressed as Tigger and Mickey Mouse and Captain Hook.

The point of the exercise was to experience one of the

world's best-known brands first hand. We spent half the day in costume, shaking hands and greeting kids and their parents. They were thrilled (except for those two girls) to meet the characters they'd grown up with. It was an interesting exercise, but I can't say I was sad when it was over.

I spent two enjoyable years at Disney, and in that time I learned a lot about brand. I also learned that even the world's best-known brands can't afford to rest on their laurels.

In California I was lucky enough to meet John Lasseter, the man who runs Pixar. Lasseter had started out as an animator at Disney. But he felt the company had reached its artistic apex with *One Hundred and One Dalmatians*, in 1961, and since then had gotten stale. He wanted to rediscover the wit and energy that had inspired the company's classic movies. He proposed using computer animation – not for the characters, just the backgrounds – in a short film, and started work on it. However, Disney executives didn't like the idea and were unhappy he hadn't kept them in the loop, and he was fired.

Lasseter went to Lucasfilm, where he joined the graphics group and began work on a short computer-animated film that would eventually become *Toy Story*. Lucasfilm Computer Graphics was bought by Steve Jobs in 1986 and became Pixar, and Lasseter was given the job of overseeing all their films. *Toy Story*, which Lasseter had directed, had been a co-production with Disney. It made more than $361 million and revolutionized the animation industry.

In early 1998, I was at the Pixar campus outside San Francisco to look at the drawings for their upcoming movie *A Bug's Life*. We had carried the *Toy Story* merchandise in the

Disney Stores and we were going to do the same with *A Bug's Life*. For the "soft" products like T-shirts and plush toys, you don't need much lead time for the manufacturers. But the "hard" products – anything made of moulded plastic, for example – require more time to get to the market. So we were looking through their preliminary drawings so we could get designs to the manufacturers.

I talked to some of the Pixar animators and attended a meeting with Lasseter and Steve Jobs. It was already obvious that these guys were the future of animation. The atmosphere around Pixar was relaxed and inspiring. You could feel the creative spark. The company didn't have the burden of history. Mickey wasn't staring down at them as they worked. Sometimes tradition is a boon and sometimes it's a burden.

I liked the people at Pixar, I liked the culture, and I liked the fact that in record time, they had built a brilliant new brand. I admired the courage it took for Lasseter to follow his instincts even though it went against the established thinking of his employer.

Disney grew to like the same things, and in 2006 it bought Pixar – one great brand recognizing the value of another. What Disney saw in Pixar was something they were losing in their own brand: passion capital.

Lasseter was made CEO of both the Pixar and Disney animation studios, a vindication of both him and his passion capital.

What's in a Name?

There is a scene in the movie *The Social Network* where Napster founder Sean Parker (played by Justin Timberlake) turns to Mark Zuckerberg (Jesse Eisenberg) and tells him to drop the "The" from TheFacebook, his new enterprise. "Just Facebook," Parker says. "It's cleaner."

Would Facebook have been as successful if it had been called TheFacebook? Probably. But what makes a brand work returns us to the notion of alchemy. It is a combination of name, product, timing, and, well, magic.

But mostly it is the result of the work that goes into defining a creed and building a culture. Culture is what we create; brand is what the world perceives.

Lists of the world's best brands tend to feature the same familiar names: Disney, Coca-Cola, IBM, Microsoft, Apple, McDonald's, Wal-Mart. If you were to do a word association test with any of these brands, what word would you come up with? Well, the answers depend on who you are. If you're a lifelong vegan, you might say "slaughterhouse" when McDonald's is mentioned. If you were the eighteen-year-old owner of a MacBook Pro, you might respond to "IBM" with the word "sucks." A small retailer might hear "Wal-Mart" and think, "Satan." Yet millions of people equate Wal-Mart with value, Macs with reliability, and McDonald's with convenience.

For better or worse, brands elicit immediate associations. We link them to something. It is generally agreed that brand recognition is a good thing. But what does "brand" mean these days?

Your Creed, Over Time

Sometimes brands are created simply by using gimmicks. The clothing retailer FCUK (French Connection United Kingdom) would fall into this category. The name has an eye-catching appeal for its target (teenaged) market. People remember it. But what do they remember?

A brand should communicate what you stand for. Every successful brand should be backed by a set of strongly held beliefs. Apple, for example, is strongly associated with innovation. Those of us of a certain age remember that Timex watches "take a licking but keep on ticking." They were reliable and affordable.

Years ago, the advertising firm Ogilvy & Mather did a campaign for Rolls-Royce. The sell line was, "At sixty miles per hour, the loudest noise comes from the electric clock." (After hearing this, one of the Rolls engineers said, "We'll have to do something about that clock.") It was an understated way of communicating the car's luxury. And understatement was the way to reach that particular audience. The brand was implied; all that was needed was a clever way of reinforcing it.

Certain brands transcend the actual product. How many people use the word "Kleenex" for any facial tissue, or say Band-aid, Xerox, Google? Sometimes we don't even know the term *is* in fact a company. Who remembers that Rollerblade was the name of the company that manufactured in-line skates? The brand co-opted the product. And with it, much of the market.

Declaring your brand is easy: all you need is a clever marketing campaign. Building your brand demands much more.

How do you build a brand? Here are eight steps:

1. DO ONE THING WELL

Most successful brands focus on one thing. They have a clarity that makes them instantly recognizable. When Ken Thomson took over his father's empire, he streamlined its diverse businesses and focused on one industry. It is a natural instinct to want to keep growing. But growth sometimes takes a company out of its core business, and that kind of expansion can end up diluting a brand rather than expanding it.

In 2011, pharmaceutical giant GlaxoSmithKline announced that it was going to divest non-core assets that included over-the-counter products. The products they were selling had strong profiles, but because of global priorities, they "lacked focus."

Also that year, Oracle, the world's second-largest software maker, began discussions with potential buyers for its software services unit. The company had hoped for synergies when it bought the division, but discovered those synergies weren't being realized.

This is a common pattern. It's a story we've all read a hundred times. Companies acquire other brands and declare that the synergies make them a perfect fit. A few years later, when those synergies haven't materialized, the new division has become a distraction, and the company quietly divests. The acquisition/expansion only took them away from what they were good at.

Recognizing your strengths and developing them is the first step in creating a successful brand.

2. MEASURE YOUR PERFORMANCE

Great brands are built on performance. All brands need to start with a few questions. First, you have to honestly assess how well your company is performing. Are you better than most of your competitors? If not, why not? If you are leading the pack, then you need to ask how you're better and why you are better.

Measuring performance means going beyond sales figures and quotas. You can hit your figures for this month but be gone in two years. You need to look at performance over the long term.

3. KNOW YOUR COMPETITION

Great brands are built in part by understanding the market, but you need to understand the competition as well. What is their market share, their strategy? What are their strengths and weaknesses? When I took on the job of president of HMV Canada, I examined the competition in great detail. I had an advantage in that the two biggest competitors were literally steps away. But even if your competition is in China, find out who they are: who they think they are and who they really are.

It's important to anticipate new competition as well.

4. BUILD YOUR BRAND ON YOUR CREED

Your brand is essentially your creed over time. If your brand is an empty marketing exercise, it may take you down the road a ways, but at some point, you'll be found out. There is a lot of beer out there that is neither good nor bad. It's simply generic. Some of those beer companies devote massive advertising budgets to promoting brand awareness. Some of them have been very successful. But the larger companies are losing market share to smaller, more innovative companies that are making more interesting beer. At some point your product will need to stand on its own merits.

5. LOOK BEYOND COMMERCIAL GAIN

Branding has become synonymous with commercial gain. Increasingly, the world's most powerful brands are causes, not corporations. Greenpeace, Amnesty International, Doctors Without Borders, and Save the Children all have enviable brand recognition and for all the right reasons. The precursor to these is the Red Cross, the gold standard in brand recognition among humanitarian organizations. Founded in Geneva in 1863, the Red Cross has been recognized and respected internationally for almost 150 years. Its distinctive bold symbol is instantly recognizable to billions of people the world over.

Increasingly there is blurring of borders between corporate brands and cause-based brands, as people like Bill and Melinda Gates and Warren Buffett turn their attention to philanthropy. Their personal brands have often changed as a result.

The Giving Pledge, established by the Gateses and Buffett, is a promise made by wealthy people to give at least half their personal wealth to charity. More than $160 billion has been pledged. The effect of this organization has been to bring attention to philanthropy itself, and to apply subtle pressure to billionaires who haven't given much of their wealth to causes. Passion capitalists tend to be associated with causes. Sometimes they are defined by them.

6. ASK TOUGH QUESTIONS

Why do we charge more than a competitor? How is our product better? When will we find a cure for cancer? Why should I pay local workers $70 an hour when a guy in Asia will do it for $7?

Every company and every individual needs to be able to ask these kinds of questions and to try to give honest answers. The answers may not always be comforting, but you need to face these realities before you can move forward and build your brand.

7. KEEP IT SIMPLE

The world has become increasingly complex. One problem with derivatives was that so few people understood them. That didn't stop those people from buying and selling them, though. Warren Buffett famously said never to invest in something you don't understand. It's good advice. In order to have a strong brand, you need to have a grasp of every aspect of your business, and you need to be able to distill what your company stands for into something that is simple and easily communicated. To paraphrase Tolstoy, there is no greatness where there is not simplicity.

Politics provides some good examples. When Jimmy Carter, a very bright man, was president of the United States, he magnified the complexity of running the world's most powerful nation. He communicated the sense that no one could do it brilliantly, though he was doing the best he could. Carter aged noticeably in office, and the electorate aged along with him. He made them nervous.

In 1980, Carter lost the election to Ronald Reagan because Reagan was able to simplify issues and speak confidently to the electorate. He spoke in parables, reduced complex tensions to issues of good versus evil. Although critics complained that he oversimplified issues, he had a calming effect. Voters were drawn to his simple message, and he won in a landslide. Reagan was known as "the great communicator" because he was able to get his message across in simple terms.

8. GO AGAINST THE GRAIN

Great brands often seem to be products of our times. But usually they anticipate the times. The times catch up to them and they suddenly seem inevitable. But they didn't start that way. Few people predicted that we would happily pay $4 for a coffee, or that half of North America would suddenly need $80 yoga pants. Successful brands are seldom found in current trends, but can be found in the counter-trends that are on the horizon.

When Ikea was founded in 1943 by a Swedish teenager, the business model ran counter to certain economic assumptions. Who (other than a Swedish teenager, maybe) wants to assemble their own furniture? Nearly seventy years later, millions of people in more than forty countries are kneeling in their living rooms, holding those familiar Allen keys and staring at those pictographic directions spread out on the rug.

Wetting Your Whistle

Examples of great brands are numerous, but they aren't always large, well-established companies. Sometimes smaller organizations have the strongest brands.

Steam Whistle Brewing was born in 1998 when three men – Greg Taylor, Cam Heaps, and Greg Cromwell – on a canoe trip talked about their dream of returning to the beer industry. All three had been fired when the Upper Canada Brewing Company was bought by Sleeman's. Using a bank loan and private equity, they bought equipment from a Quebec brewery that was closing its doors, and set up in a historic roundhouse that had been used to service locomotives in the Toronto railyards. Embossed on the bottom of each of the distinctive green Steam Whistle bottles is "3FG," which stands for "3 Fired Guys."

Taylor, Heaps, and Cromwell started their microbrewery with two aims: to brew the most respected Pilsner in the country, and to be sustainable. The brewery's volume is relatively small (120,000 barrels in 2011), but their reputation has grown. In 2004, they were voted best locally produced beer in Toronto. The following year, they were named Ontario's Best Pilsner.

The company's motto is: "Do one thing really, really well." When asked about their goal, they said it was less about volume than reputation. By 2006, sales put them in the "Top Ten selling premium beers" in Ontario Beer Stores. In a few years, they had established a brand that was known for uncompromising quality.

Their efforts at sustainability include using all-natural

ingredients in their beer and using bottles that can be recycled three times more than industry-standard bottles. They use deep-water cooling from Lake Ontario rather than air conditioning in the summer, and their trucks are fuelled with biodiesel made from soya oil and recycled restaurant grease. They were the first brewery in Canada to adopt compostable beer cups. They have showers, towel service, and safe bike storage to encourage employees to cycle to work, and the food that is left over from events at their historic site goes to a local street mission. Since 2005 they have had an employee profit-sharing program.

The founders of Steam Whistle had a passion for making beer, and it has translated into a recognizable brand that is synonymous with quality and sustainability. What had been a passion for the product when they worked for another brewery was translated into passion capital when they started their own.

Running Away to Join the Circus

In 1984, the circus was a dying art form. It was being killed by indifference, and to a lesser extent by animal rights groups protesting against the treatment of the bears, lions, elephants, and dogs that laboured under the Big Top.

Quebec's Guy Laliberté energized the form by getting rid of the animals, adapting street performance, adding original music, and developing themes for the shows. The performers got more ambitious, as did the productions. The shows developed a following.

Laliberté started his career as a stilt-walking, fire-eating, accordion-playing street busker. These three skills tend not to be prized in the corporate world. But as the founder and CEO of Cirque du Soleil, Laliberté is now personally worth $2.5 billion. His circus employs four thousand people from more than forty countries.

A century ago, circuses didn't have a theme. They were a collection of spectacles. If you didn't like one spectacle, another one came along in a few minutes. What circuses had then, more than anything else, was novelty. You couldn't see anything like it anywhere else. The circus was an exotic spectacle.

But today, with TV and the Internet, spectacle is everywhere, and the competition for the entertainment dollar is fierce and diverse. The traditional circus didn't have a narrative, it didn't have a story. Every time it came to town, it was essentially the same.

So how did Laliberté turn what was essentially a nineteenth-century form of entertainment into the hot ticket on five continents? He understood that what had made the circus such a popular event for so many years was the drama and magic that surrounded it. Would the trapeze artist fall? Would the lion close his mouth on the lion tamer's head? But the modern circus had lost most of its mystery. The drama was generic. The animals were tired. The lighting, music, and clowns were tired.

Like Ken Thomson, Laliberté realized what he was actually selling. Thomson knew it wasn't books and newspapers but knowledge and information. Laliberté knew it wasn't clowns on bicycles but drama and mystery.

By basing each new Cirque creation on a specific theme, Laliberté brought freshness and meaning to his shows. He reinvented a genre, and in the process he created a powerful brand where we know what to expect, but we also know we will see the unexpected. Each show breaks new ground.

Laliberté's philanthropic forays use the circus as springboard. He gave $100 million to One Drop, which is devoted to giving everyone in the world access to water. The initiative was inspired by Cirque du Monde, which is Cirque du Soleil's international program for street children.

Emerging Markets, Emerging Brands

You may not have heard of Tata Motors, but it has annual revenues of more than $20 billion and employs fifty thousand people. It is the largest car manufacturer in India. And India is one of the two fastest-developing markets in the world.

Tata began by manufacturing locomotives in 1945. Nine years later it produced a commercial car in a joint venture with Daimler-Benz of Germany. Other cars were produced by Tata, but it wasn't until 1998 that it launched the Indica, India's first indigenous small passenger car. It was a huge success, and Tata became the bestselling brand in India. Ten years later, in a symbolic colonial reversal, Tata acquired Jaguar and Land Rover, the iconic British brands.

Foreign carmakers weren't looking very closely at India, in part because its poverty levels were so high. Who could afford their cars? And the infrastructure was so poor that it couldn't support many cars. There wasn't a well-developed system of highways, and what roads did exist were often cheaply built and poorly maintained. (The first trucks Tata manufactured with Daimler were too heavy for the roads, so they had to adapt their design.)

But India is a democracy with high levels of education and literacy, and it has an emerging middle class. A demographic is forming, a powerful demographic that wants a car and is capable of buying one. What was needed for the market was a car that was very small (to deal with the impossibly clogged roads) and very inexpensive. The Indica was designed with precisely those issues in mind.

The failure to understand and predict how India would develop cost some foreign auto manufacturers a piece of a growing market. Tata captured not just the market but the hearts and minds of the Indian consumer and then took their brand to Thailand, Indonesia, Sri Lanka, and Africa, going after other emerging markets.

The introduction of an even cheaper car, the Nano, was largely expected to be a triumph. It was both extremely cheap (US$2,500) and well engineered. But Tata didn't nurture the brand. There wasn't much advertising for the Nano, and the car became associated with cheapness rather than economy. When a few Nanos burst into flames, the company didn't address the situation with a PR offensive, and consumers were rattled. Tata also failed to provide on-site financing for their customers, most of whom would need to borrow in order to buy the car.

The Nano was innovative, and came on the heels of strong brand awareness, but Tata's complacency cost them. They were hoping to sell 25,000 Nanos a month; a year after the launch, they sold 1,200 in one month. Complacency is a threat to even the strongest brand.

The Real Thing, the Pepsi Challenge, and the Laughing Baby

Both Coke and Pepsi did anticipate the emerging market in China. Coca-Cola got an early foothold in China, setting up a bottling plant in 1927, though it left in 1949 when the Communists took power. In 1979, Coca-Cola was the first U.S. company to sell its products when Deng Xiaoping opened China to foreign investment. It has grown its business through expansion and strategic partnerships with both government and domestic companies, and China is now Coke's third-largest market, after the United States and Mexico.

PepsiCo arrived in China a little later – in 1982 – and quickly grew to rival Coke for market share. Over the course of the next decade, the two American giants successfully muscled out most of the domestic competition, claiming almost 90 per cent of the soft drink market.

But the fastest-growing drink manufacturer in the country is the Chinese company Hangzhou Wahaha Group. (The name Wahaha is the sound of a baby laughing and was taken from a children's folk song.) Founded in 1987, Wahaha produces bottled water, iced tea, fruit drinks, and Future Cola. It didn't start making its own cola until 1998. Before going after the cola giants, Wahaha examined its strengths. It was able to make a cola whose taste was almost indistinguishable from Coke or Pepsi. But since all the ingredients were local, their

Future Cola was cheaper to manufacture and could be sold for less. And because it was a domestic brand, Wahaha was able to design an advertising campaign that appealed to Chinese patriotism ("China's cola").

Wahaha initially targeted the huge rural market, which both Coke and Pepsi had ignored. That market is poor and scattered, and distribution costs in China are high, so Wahaha had it largely to itself. The cola giants understandably preferred the incredibly concentrated markets in the major cities (China has sixteen cities with populations of more than ten million). But the urban supermarkets have high stocking fees that both Coke and Pepsi are obliged to pay, cutting into their bottom line. China, however, is going through the largest urbanization in history. At some point those people who grew up drinking Wahaha on their farm will live in the cities, and they may stick with Future Cola. The plan of selling in rural areas is a long-term strategy, something at which China excels.

Within a decade Future Cola had almost reached the market share of its American rivals. The fourth quarter of 2010 saw a decline of 3 per cent in Coke sales in China for the first time. Meanwhile, Wahaha continues to grow.

China's soft drink market is currently worth US$49 billion. By 2015, it is projected to grow to $86 billion. Wahaha is growing not just in the lucrative Chinese market but abroad. Wahaha products are now distributed in the United States, France, Germany, and Italy, among other countries. Like Tata, it is engaging the enemy on its home turf.

Controlling the Narrative of Your Brand

When Johnson & Johnson was hit with the Tylenol scare in 1982 and seven people died, the brand association with "Tylenol" was at a dangerous crossroads. Would a pain reliever be associated with death? When J&J decisively withdrew the product and offered free replacements, they essentially wrote their own narrative. Rather than tragedy, Tylenol became associated with corporate responsibility.

A brand is a narrative. Sometimes companies lose track of their own story, or let their story be determined by others. Sometimes they are haunted by what a brand once stood for. Brands aren't static. That narrative can quickly change, can become a burden.

We saw it with Disney and with General Motors, to name two brands with a long tradition that lost their way. Culture is what is created within a company, and it's what insiders see; brand is what the world sees, and it is free to interpret it however it likes. Wal-Mart has been perceived in many communities as a rapacious force that kills local business. They have tried to rewrite that narrative by becoming a green company. In 2006, CEO H. Lee Scott Jr. announced that Wal-Mart was working toward running on renewable energy and producing zero waste. The green initiative is Wal-Mart's attempt to take control of its own narrative.

Brand represents the work that goes into creating a creed and growing a culture. It's crucial to control your own narrative.

Can Real Life Be Branded?

Reality TV is ubiquitous these days. It has become the dominant genre in television because it's cheap to produce and because there is an audience for it. There are dozens of series, though many of them are indistinguishable. One of the few shows that still manages to stand out is *Survivor*, which debuted in the summer of 2000. For the next six years it remained one of the top ten highest-rated shows on television. In 2009, *Entertainment Weekly* named the show the No. 1 reality series of all time. *Survivor* defined reality TV. Getting "voted off the island" entered the language, a triumph for any brand.

The show was produced by Mark Burnett, who went on to produce *The Apprentice*, *Are You Smarter Than a 5th Grader?* and *The Voice*, among other shows. In the thousand-channel universe, one that is heavily freighted with reality shows, he has created a recognizable brand for the genre. In 2004, *Time* named Burnett one of the 100 most influential people in the world.

Trumping Yourself

In the wake of his success with *Survivor*, Burnett met Donald Trump, who said they should do a series together. The next time Burnett was in New York, he called Trump to say he was working on an idea but it wasn't ready yet. Trump told him to come in and pitch it anyway. Burnett did, worried that he hadn't really thought it through. He made the pitch, and the famously decisive Trump said, "I like it, let's do it." He told his assistant to get his agent on the phone and get a contract drawn up.

Burnett spoke briefly to Trump's agent, who was furious that he hadn't been in the room when the deal was struck. He listened to Burnett pitch his idea once more over the phone, then said he didn't like it and he was going to advise Trump not to do it. Burnett went back to Trump and told him about the call. Trump bellowed for his assistant to get the agent back on the phone. Trump picked up the phone and said, "You're fired!" and hung up.

Burnett had just found the tag line for his new show.

The Apprentice not only extended Burnett's personal brand but also went a long way to defining Trump's brand. Burnett's belief that a new kind of TV show could be successful, rejecting the established parameters of prime-time viewing, changed the TV landscape.

A Good Brand Can Ignite Passion

Most romantic relationships begin with passion. But as many married people (and most divorced people) know, it can fade. Passion capital is no different. A company built on passion may be successful, but eventually it can become complacent. Brands lose their heart.

When the Gap came on the scene, it projected an image of hipness and accessibility. Their product line wasn't radical, but it was distinctive. Their commercials enlisted celebrities, but not always the ones you'd expect. They were sometimes older (Kris Kristofferson, Mia Farrow) or quirkier. Occasionally, they were dead (James Dean). The brand was instantly recognizable, and was cool to more than one generation.

The Gap captured a market and ruled it for years, but it rested on its laurels. Sales slumped, and its share price struggled. It had become the establishment, dangerous territory for what was essentially an anti-establishment brand. Being the establishment is good if you're a bank, but it isn't good for every business.

In contrast, Apple has done well by remaining the innovative counterculture alternative. It isn't always easy to maintain the image of a rebel when your company has a market cap of more than $300 billion, but Apple has managed it brilliantly. (Their "Hi, I'm a Mac. And I'm a PC" ads have reinforced this idea.) Apple has retained and built on its passion capital.

It can be a challenge to remain passionate, whether it's in business or in a relationship. Passion is a garden that needs constant tending. Don't take it for granted, because when it's gone, it is very difficult to recapture.

Before the 2010 Winter Olympics in Vancouver, Canada had hosted the Olympic games twice: the 1976 Summer Olympics in Montreal and the 1988 Winter Olympics in Calgary. Canada became the first country to have hosted multiple Olympics without winning a gold medal. In 2004, several Canadian amateur sports associations met to discuss their goals for the 2010 Games. The result was the Own the Podium program.

It was a brash title, certainly un-Canadian in its boldness. It also had the chance to backfire, given Canada's past record as host. What if Canada failed to win a gold yet again?

The goal for OTP was for the country to be the top winter sporting nation in the world by 2010. Canada has lots of winter, but it doesn't have lots of people. Critics said this goal was unrealistic. The OTP plan stressed preparation, technology, and research into human performance. Elite athletes were identified and supported.

Meanwhile, the phrase "Own the Podium" caught on with the public. It branded the Vancouver Games. Even better, the program also succeeded in getting Canadians to the podium. In 2010, Canada won fourteen golds, the most any country had ever won in a winter Olympics.

The OTP brand was a risk, but it was one that paid off. The reason the branding was successful was because the program concentrated on the culture of sport – it supported the elite athletes. The Own the Podium program was founded on a strongly held belief that was backed by a change in culture and the courage to make that statement to the world.

The term "Brand X" is usually given to brands that aren't referred to by name but are implied to be of inferior quality compared to the brand that is being advertised. The term became so entrenched that it was co-opted by a jazz band (which occasionally featured Phil Collins on drums), a punk band, and, unsurprisingly, an advertising agency. Brand X has itself become a brand.

Anything can become a brand. But it is important to remember that a brand must stand for something. It is the logical product of a creed that inspired a culture. We can manufacture brands based on clever marketing campaigns, and many have, but this kind of branding is superficial and isn't a recipe for longevity. Lasting brands are built on creed, culture, and courage.

KEY LESSONS

1. Your brand is your reputation. As Jeff Bezos said, "You earn reputation by trying to do hard things well."

2. Your brand is built over time and represents a promise of performance.

3. Great brands take on some of the passion associated with great causes. Likewise, great causes can learn from the performance of great brands.

4. Your brand is your unique proposition built on creed, culture, and courage.

5. Great brands are created by going against the grain or transforming the status quo.

6

RESOURCES:

MARSHALLING AND MASTERING

Who can exhaust a man? Who knows a man's resources?
JEAN-PAUL SARTRE

In the business world, the resources we usually talk about are financial, human, and intellectual. Of these, financial resources are what most companies concentrate on: how to attract them, find them, generate them. But to concentrate solely on financial resources is a mistake. Money is critical to any business, but we risk forgetting how important the other resources are. And money doesn't flow into a vacuum. It follows other resources.

Whether its business, politics, or life, we all start with certain resources. It is key to understand what they are and how best to allocate them.

In 2006 both President George Bush and his nemesis Venezuelan president Hugo Chávez were in New York speaking at the United Nations. It was a year after Hurricane

Katrina, and Bush was trying to do some damage control after being accused of negligence, while Chávez was there to take advantage politically.

Chávez told a gathering of peace and anti-globalization activists and community and religious leaders that he would supply America's poor with oil now that Louisiana's refineries were crippled. It was an irony that the media couldn't resist: the socialist president offering to take care of the world's richest country. "The world cannot tolerate this model of development called the American way of life," Chávez had earlier told the UN Assembly, to general applause.

Billed as the successful oilman versus the unsuccessful oilman, the battle between Bush and Chávez continued in the press over the next few days. Chávez told *Time*, "Bush wanted Iraq's oil and I believe he wants Venezuela's oil. But the blame for high prices lies in the consumer model of the U.S. Its reckless oil consumption is a form of suicide."

What resources were at issue in this scenario?

First, of course, there was oil. Venezuela is the fifth-largest exporter of crude to the United States, supplying roughly 878,000 barrels a day in 2011. The United States is grateful for the oil and Venezuela desperately needs the business. Chávez had a point in that American consumerism as a model for the world is a form of suicide (the United States has 4.5 per cent of the world's people and consumes more than 25 per cent of its energy). But Chávez would likely be happier if the United States consumed *more* oil; it would be good for Venezuela.

But the bickering over oil was largely a sideshow. The second resource here was financial capital. America remains the world's richest country; Venezuela was ranked fifty-ninth by the International Monetary Fund. The idea that Venezuela was in effect offering to send foreign aid to the States in the form of oil was a wonderful irony. Except it didn't actually happen. It too was a sideshow.

The most critical resource in the skirmish between Bush and Chávez was political capital. Chávez called Bush "the devil" in the UN Assembly, and the footage was replayed on state-run TV networks in Venezuela for days, proof to Venezuelans that their leader had denounced the world's most powerful man right in his own backyard. Chávez didn't jeopardize Venezuela's business relationship with the United States – the financial capital was never at risk. Oil was the window dressing here; politics was the true resource.

At the time, political capital held more value to both men than either oil or money. Bush was at his lowest ebb in the polls, with a post-Katrina approval rating of 40 per cent. Chávez was popular with Venezuela's poor, but his many critics claimed he was mismanaging the country's primary resource, oil. The country was divided on his leadership.

At any given moment, certain resources have inherently more worth than others. The formula is rarely static. You need people or ideas or money or time. But what you need most changes from month to month.

"Scarcity of resources" is heard every day as we face rapid population growth and dwindling resources. Will we run out of oil? Or water? Where is the price of copper going? Or gold or potash? Canada is resource-rich, an enviable thing as we move through the twenty-first century. Resources can mean life or death. They can mean life or death in business as well.

Dressing for Success

Harry Rosen started a menswear store with his brother Lou in 1954 in an unlikely part of Toronto known as Cabbagetown, essentially the Irish ghetto. The store was small (500 square feet) and the location wasn't ideal, but Rosen knew his business depended more on relationships than location. Rosen is a prime example of someone who had few financial resources but great personal resources: the ability to bring people together, to engender loyalty in staff, customers, and suppliers. It took seven years for him to be able to afford a larger store in a better location. When he moved, it was initially to the financial district, where most of his market was. It was a move that met with skepticism – the high-end stores were all located elsewhere. But the move paid off.

As the store gained traction, Rosen forged relationships with some of the world's great brands – Zegna, Hugo Boss, Armani. Ermenegildo Zegna, grandson of the Italian company's founder, said, "From Harry I learned many of the skills of a fine merchant." Today, Harry Rosen's fifteen stores account for 30 per cent of the high-end menswear sold in Canada.

For more than fifty years, Rosen has accommodated changing fashions in menswear. He understood that the key to his business wasn't lapel widths or pant styles, but relationships.

His son Larry, now the CEO, has shown an adept touch at marshalling resources and has become a powerful new leader in menswear. He expanded the flagship store, which is now regarded as one of the finest menswear stores in the world. He has inherited a tradition of passion capital and built on it.

Financial Capital Follows Passion Capital

How do investors make decisions? They evaluate a company's profit and loss statements. They look at the sector, examine debt levels. They use sophisticated models and technical analysis; they look at Fibonacci numbers, volume analysis, and candlestick charts. While these are all helpful tools, they weren't much use when the stock market took a dive in 2008.

Among the banks that took a beating was Citibank, which saw its share price cut in half in just four days. In February 2009, its CEO, Vikram Pandit, announced that he would work for a dollar a year without a bonus until the bank returned to profitability. In a sense, he had reduced one of the largest banks in America to a start-up: he wouldn't make money until it did. The market responded, and money flowed back to the bank. During the third quarter of 2009, there were nineteen days when Citibank shares traded more than a billion times as traders jumped on board. At a time when executive compensation was a hot-button issue, Pandit defused it, and reduced the issue of management to one of passion rather than perks.

Money is constantly in motion – billions move around the globe daily looking for a lucrative place to land. What is it drawn to? In a 2010 survey by the National Venture Capital Association, 60 per cent of its members responded that energy would be the biggest draw. Next to that were medical devices.

One of the medical devices that was funded by venture capital in 2011 was a hybrid walker-wheelchair designed by nineteen-year-old Gary Kurek, of Bonnyville, Alberta, a small town north of Edmonton. Kurek started designing mobility devices when his grandparents were diagnosed with cancer and his aunt with Lou Gehrig's disease. He had always excelled at science fairs and now he had a specific focus for his talents. He approached the problem – making their quality of life better – with the passion of someone who has a personal stake.

As a result of his success with a prototype for the walker-wheelchair, Kurek received a $100,000 grant from Peter Thiel, the co-founder of PayPal. Thiel runs a venture capital fund, the Thiel Foundation, that identifies successful start-ups. In 2011, twenty-four fellowships were awarded to people under the age of twenty who had come up with compelling start-up ideas.

Thiel, an American who was born in Germany, believes that the United States has lost the innovative spark that made the country great. It's hard to disagree with him. Its people are still innovative, but the corporate culture is letting them down. Corporate America is held hostage to short-term goals, and innovation demands a longer timeline. So Thiel puts his resources behind individuals who he believes are innovative.

A *New York Times* article in May 2011 cited a 1961 Chevrolet-sponsored movie trailer. The image was of boys building a sandcastle. "Of all things Americans are, we are makers," said the voice-over. "With our strengths and our minds and spirit, we gather, we form, and we fashion: makers and shapers and put-it-togetherers." That spirit quietly disappeared, but the article argued that it might be resurging, that Americans would once more be makers and shapers.

Money has to flow somewhere. The dismal era of wringing more money out of increasingly complex investment instruments has waned. Certain sectors – the automotive sector, for one – have paid a steep price for not being innovative. We in North America seem to be learning a lesson. Money is slowly beginning to follow passion.

Human Capital Flows toward Passion Capital

The act of creating something is the result of passion, whether it's writing computer code or a novel. Cities that are centres for creativity tend to build a critical mass; creativity follows creativity.

A century ago, people simply followed the job market. In the 1920s, thousands of people went to Detroit to work in the auto industry. But that industry contracted, and today Detroit has half the population that it did at its peak in 1950. In the nineteenth century, Buffalo was a shipping and manufacturing centre that attracted a lot of immigrants, but it lost its shipping business and the industries moved elsewhere. Buffalo now has fewer people than it had in 1900. Once-thriving cities like Cleveland and St. Louis have similar histories.

Manufacturing centres are at the mercy of the market for their specific products. If that market declines or disappears, the industry tends to do the same. But if the market booms, that can present new problems. It may become cheaper to manufacture offshore, and the local jobs disappear. Some of the newly unemployed leave to find work elsewhere. "Write if you get work" is the classic catchphrase of traditional capitalism.

But a new paradigm is forming in which companies are moving to cities that nurture creativity. In his books *The Rise of the Creative Class* and *Cities and the Creative Class*, Richard Florida argues that creativity is a critical component of the twenty-first-century economy, and people flock to places that nurture and accommodate creativity. Toronto, Silicon Valley, San Francisco, Austin, Los Angeles, and New York are all examples.

Creative people flock to these cities, and companies follow the people to draw on a workforce. Unlike the example of Detroit in the 1920s, though, the people are coming for more than just jobs. They are looking for an environment that is amenable to their lifestyle. In the traditional model, which we still see in boomtowns, workers will put up with over-priced, often substandard accommodation in return for high wages. But knowledge workers are seeking an environment of like-minded people. That's why there are clusters like Silicon Valley.

Even within the cities themselves, human capital is dictating where the companies are locating. In Toronto, a lot of businesses moved to the suburbs during the recession of the 1990s because rents there were cheaper and taxes were lower. The downtown once held the lion's share of large and mid-sized business, but by 2000 the balance had shifted. Toronto's suburbs had the second-highest number of Canadian head offices, next to Calgary, and significantly more than down-town Toronto.

But the recession of 2008 saw companies moving back to the core. According to CB Richard Ellis Canada, a real estate consultancy firm, commercial vacancy rates in the fourth quarter of 2010 were higher in the Toronto suburbs than in the downtown core. Yet the downtown rents were still higher (on average by $6.50 a square foot). Why would companies return to downtown, and pay higher rent, during a severe recession?

The answer is that a cultural change happened in the past decade. Knowledge-based industries that had survived 2008 in pretty good shape were buying or renting more space in the core. According to John O'Toole, executive vice-president of CBRE, "It's all about retention and attraction of employees."

The best and brightest employees under thirty didn't want to work (or live) in the suburbs, regardless of salary. They preferred a workplace they could walk, bike, or take public transit to. They wanted the amenities of the downtown core. They calculated the expense, lost time, and soul-deadening effects of a commute in ways their predecessors didn't. They attached value to their time. They saw it both qualitatively and quantitatively – as a resource. To keep these people, employers either moved back to the core or expanded existing facilities there.

The history of traditional capitalism – not always an uplifting history – has been one of supply and demand. Usually labour is desperate to fill whatever jobs are available, and so workers put up with poor conditions, long commutes, low pay. But another model has emerged, one in which knowledge-based industries, which aren't wedded to resources or specific locations, or even bricks and mortar, simply search for the most fertile soil. There is less hierarchy, more fluidity, and greater mobility. Increasing numbers of people are following ideas and cultures; they are following passion capital.

Marshalling Resources

Here are five recommended concepts to help make effective and efficient use of scarce resources to create passion capital:

1. THE "THREE RIGHTS"

Understand the three "right" decisions that need to be made in all resource-allocation decisions. The three resource decisions are:

i) select the right resource (financial, human, intellectual, technological, or some combination of these resources),

ii) invest in the right place (decide if you are addressing a supply chain problem or a training issue), and

iii) invest at the right time (timing can be the most difficult resource-allocation decision).

Making the right decisions on these three important aspects of resource allocation is the starting point to marshalling resources for building passion capital.

2. SUFFICIENCY

Conventional wisdom says that the more resources allocated to an opportunity, the better. However, sufficiency means different things to different organizations at different stages of their development. Start-ups often make resource decisions that are wasteful because of insufficiency, and large, established firms often make wasteful resource decisions because of excessive resource allocation.

3. SCARCITY

Most small businesses and start-ups struggle with scarce financial and human resources. Yet these small firms might have intellectual or technological capital in great abundance. The reality is that a nearly limitless supply of all resources is available to those who understand how to create passion capital. Inability to gather and direct resources is the result of weaknesses in one or more of the seven principles of passion capital, not the result of insufficient resources. Venture capitalists and merchant bankers worldwide bemoan the lack of "great investment ideas," while entrepreneurs complain about the lack of financing. Scarcity is the result of lack of passion capital and in particular, one or more of its building blocks.

4. OWNERSHIP

If every person responsible for making resource decisions acts like an owner, then effective and efficient use of resources will result. When it's your money, you take greater care in how it's spent. No one ever puts premium gas in a rental car. Building a sense of ownership is one certain way of making better resource decisions.

5. DEBTORS BEWARE

Easy access to seemingly cheap credit has led many companies and households to make disastrous resource decisions. Borrowing to start, expand, or improve a business or a career is often necessary, but debt can be one of the most dangerous and costly of all resources. Debt can force decisions that kill passion capital. The burden of debt kills more careers and companies than lack of financial capital. It's amazing what those with passion capital can accomplish even in the absence of financial resources, in particular financial resources secured through debt. If you want passion capital, "owe not."

Intellectual Capital Follows Passion Capital

We associate intellectual capital with innovation. You would expect that the company with the greatest resources would come up with the most innovations. But Facebook was developed by a few Harvard students. Google should have come from a corporation like Microsoft, but it was the product of two Stanford students. Bell or AT&T should have developed handheld email communications devices, but it was an engineering student from the University of Waterloo.

Large companies have vast stores of both financial and human capital. But intellectual capital comes from inspiration. It's the guy in his basement who invents the new app or builds the better mousetrap. Intellectual capital is driven by the passion of individuals.

Both Stanford University and the University of Waterloo figured in the list above. Stanford has been called the incubator of Silicon Valley. Among the tech companies that have spun out of Stanford are Hewlett-Packard, Sun Microsystems, Cisco Systems, and Silicon Graphics. These companies in turn spun out others: Hewlett-Packard people went on to start Apple Computer, Compaq, and Siemens. More than a thousand small companies and upwards of a hundred large ones have come directly out of Stanford and put tens of billions of dollars into the economy.

In Canada, the University of Waterloo is the centre of the country's Technology Triangle, which incorporates the cities of Waterloo, Kitchener, and Cambridge. More than 250 tech companies, including Open Text, Canada's largest software company, got their start at the University of Waterloo.

Why have Stanford and Waterloo had such high rates of success with tech start-ups?

One thing these two institutions have in common is that they allow both students and staff to retain the patents on anything they develop while associated with the university (unlike the University of Toronto or Harvard, among others). This policy may seem counterintuitive. At first glance it would seem to be in the university's interest to retain ownership of those ideas, to amass intellectual capital rather than forgo it.

But leaving the rights in the hands of the creator provides more initiative to create. So more patents are developed, more companies formed. And the university derives benefits from the successful companies and the alumni those companies nurture.

Intellectual capital is the result of passion: someone has an idea and they pursue it single-mindedly. The tech start-ups are examples of intellectual capital following passion capital.

Buying Passion Capital

Passion capital isn't a commodity. You can't buy it. But that doesn't stop people from trying. A large company that either never possessed passion capital or has somehow lost it some-times tries to regain it by buying a smaller company that does have it. It's a familiar pattern.

In 2005, Cadbury, the venerable British chocolate manu-facturer, swallowed up small organic chocolate maker Green & Black's. Cadbury was a successful company that had a reputation as a good chocolate maker. It's not that their reputation had declined, but the definition of what consti-tuted good chocolate changed dramatically in a decade. The growing success of high-end Belgian and Swiss brands, the successful launch of small, organic chocolatiers, and the emergence of fair-trade products changed the landscape. By 2007, artisanal chocolate was the fastest-growing segment of the industry. Cadbury went from "good" to simply "generic" without anything changing in the company. It was the market that shifted.

The takeover of G&B lent Cadbury a certain cachet, and it was a hedge against the growing high-end organic choco-late market. People were prepared to spend more on or-ganic, fair-trade chocolate, and Cadbury ensured it could take advantage of that trend by buying a recognized leader. But in 2010 Cadbury was itself swallowed up by Kraft in a hostile takeover.

Whatever fears existed in the first takeover – that Green & Black's would lose its soul, that its quality would suffer – were now magnified. Cadbury was at least a chocolate manufac-turer; Kraft was the food equivalent of Wal-Mart. Instead of G&B's passion infusing Kraft, the organic chocolate maker's passion was in danger of being compromised or deadened by its parent company.

In 2005 that is what happened when chocolate giant Hershey took over the small chocolate company Scharffen Berger. Started in a Berkeley, California, kitchen by a doctor and a winemaker, Scharffen Berger was an early success in the artisanal chocolate market. When Hershey bought it for a reported $50 million, they did what takeover companies usually do: they reassured customers that the quality would remain intact. Only it didn't. Chocolate aficionados quickly reported a difference in the new chocolate bars. They noticed a chalky texture. "It was becoming just another mediocre American chocolate," one fan noted. In acquiring Scharffen Berger, Hershey was trying to buy passion capital. Instead, the passion capital was dissipated.

Kraft's experience with Green & Black's wasn't much different. Customers who were fans of G&B were justifiably skittish after the takeover, and Kraft gained few, if any, public relations points from its association with an organic, fair-trade product.

If this was purely a bottom-line acquisition, then the larger distribution networks may or may not make up for a loss in core consumers. But the passion capital is diminished rather than expanded; it has been subsumed by a conglomerate. In this case, the conglomerate often doesn't gain, but the company built on passion capital loses. Passion capital can be squandered. It can disappear if it isn't nurtured.

Watering the Wine

Most wineries begin as a labour of love. Winemaking is a capital- and labour-intensive business, and it is filled with people who have a passion for wine. When Robert Mondavi started his winery in 1966 in California's Napa Valley, American wines had a poor reputation, even though there had been vineyards there for a century. The resources in California were extraordinary: they had the right climate, the right soil, and plenty of capital. Yet the wines that came out of the Napa Valley were almost exclusively low-end products that didn't have any presence outside the United States. Mondavi wanted to create a wine that rivalled the great labels of Europe.

By 1979 he had developed a premium label, and then he entered into a co-production with the prestigious French winery Château Mouton Rothschild to create Opus One, a critically acclaimed high-end winery. By 1997, his wine empire had grown well past the borders of California, and he achieved the recognition he wanted for American wines: his Chardonnay Reserve was ranked top wine by the Grand European Jury Wine Tasting that year.

Robert Mondavi was a charismatic man whose drive to make great wines not only made his own winery a success, it helped put California wines on the world stage. The industry grew from a glorified hobby to a $30-billion industry in Mondavi's lifetime, and he played a large part in that development.

Mondavi's passion didn't flag, but his passion capital did. As Robert Mondavi Wines grew, it bought up smaller wineries, but with these acquisitions, it also acquired a lot of debt. In addition, there was ongoing internal turmoil. Mondavi's two sons were part of the company, and he pitted himself against them at times, and pitted them against one another as well. He publicly criticized them for emphasizing the less expensive lines – Coastal and Woodbridge – after the company had spent so much time cultivating the premium brands. He said it would take time for the company to recover its image.

But the inexpensive lines were the financial engine for the company. Winemaking is capital-intensive, and Robert's quest for perfection was drawing a lot of money out of the company. In 1993, the company went public in an effort to raise money to deal with its debt, which had reached $126 million. It was a move that some critics warned against, saying the company would need to pursue expansion and profit at the expense of quality.

The prediction came true. Mondavi's premium wines had regularly made the Top 10 lists of California cabernets, but soon his wines were notoriously missing. What happened? As one critic noted, "Along the way, the Mondavi winery's original reason for being, a commitment to quality wine, succumbed to a desire for profits above all."

By 2004, Mondavi was pictured as the bad guy in a wine documentary titled *Mondovino*. The film was directed by a former sommelier named Jonathan Nossiter who argued that Mondavi's acquisition of small wineries in Italy and in Bordeaux threatened their quality. The irony was that Mondavi had once been that small producer infused with passion for great wine. Now he was being cast as the globalizing villain who would try to squeeze more profit from these small vineyards by making their wines more accessible and less individualistic. They would no longer express their terroir, but instead express the bottom line.

To make matters worse, Mondavi's debts became insurmountable. His own financial health was wrapped up in shares of the company, and much of it was earmarked for charity. When the stock price fell, his fortune fell as well, and he was worried he wouldn't be able to honour his charitable pledges. In 2004, he sold his company to Constellation, the largest drinks conglomerate in the world, for $1.36 billion; Constellation assumed all debt. Mondavi's passion capital evaporated in a cloud of debt and globalization.

Robert Mondavi died in 2008 at the age of ninety-four, a good advertisement for the health benefits of wine. "He was a true California legend," Governor Arnold Schwarzenegger said after Mondavi died. "It is hard to imagine anyone having more of a lasting impact on California's $30-billion wine industry than Robert Mondavi."

Mondavi was an inspirational figure, but his was also a cautionary tale. In the wake of the sale to Constellation, Mondavi and his sons became wealthy, but they were also angry and frustrated that their extraordinary empire had disappeared. Passion capital needs to be nurtured and tended. In the case of the Mondavi winery, Robert never lost his passion, but he lost his passion capital, and with it, finally, his company.

His two sons have now started a new winery, Continuum, which is infused with the original spirit that Mondavi brought to the Napa Valley. It's unlikely they will make the same mistakes. They want to recapture the passion capital that their father built.

Resource Play

Sometimes the passion that built a smaller company does energize larger companies. We saw evidence of this in the oil business thirty years ago, when T. Boone Pickens aggressively pursued takeover targets that were larger than his own company.

In some ways, Pickens is the quintessential American oilman. He started his first oil company with $2,500 while in his twenties. That eventually grew into Mesa Petroleum, a $2-billion company, the largest independent in the country.

Despite his wealth and success, Pickens maintained the stance of the outsider, and he shook up the boardrooms of the nation and put a scare into Big Oil. He wanted to inject some of his passion into what he saw as a complacent culture. But he also wanted to make money. His strategy was to invest in corporations he liked, then publicly proclaim that he could run them better than existing management. He then bitterly fought for control of the company, and usually lost the battle. But he made money as an investor when his takeover sold to another, more friendly bidder at a high price.

These tactics earned him the ire of many in the industry. But his other stated objective was to make the large oil companies more responsive to their shareholders. He pointed out that most CEOs in Big Oil held relatively few shares of their own companies (an average of 0.03 per cent at the time) and didn't have anything at stake. He accused them of simply being overpriced hired hands. In short, they lacked passion. His aim was to inject some of the passion of the independents into big companies like Chevron and Mobil. His critics (and there were a lot of them) said he was only out to benefit himself.

Perhaps, but he was an innovative leader of his own company. In 1979, he built a $2.5-million, thirty-thousand-square-foot fitness centre at Mesa, with the idea that healthier employees would translate into healthier profits. He extended memberships to the families of his employees – an initiative that some companies are just coming to now. He placed a high value on human capital, and included the employees in his passion. "Make sure as many people as possible have a stake in the game," he once said.

In his personality and tactics, Pickens was the direct opposite of the quiet, gentlemanly Ken Thomson. But both men shared certain philosophies. They both put a premium on attracting and holding on to good people. They both understood that you need to take the long-term perspective. And they could both see the larger picture. Pickens was an oilman, but he was really in the energy business. "My No. 1 issue is security," he once said. "I want off OPEC oil. We're buying from the enemy and we're paying for both sides of the war. I don't like to look stupid. And we look stupid."

In the 1980s the United States still had lots of oil reserves, so it made sense to be an oilman. But those resources have diminished and there is greater dependence on foreign oil. Pickens pointed out that in March 2011 the United States imported 72 per cent of its oil – 348 million barrels – which sent about $39.9 billion to foreign countries. He calculated it at $922,912 per minute. His solution was to take advantage of the extensive natural gas reserves in the States, which could last more than a century at current consumption levels. A third of the country's oil goes into transportation, with the largest slice going to power heavy trucks. He advocated switching to a natural gas fleet.

He also planned to spend up to $1 billion on wind farms in Texas. His plan is to use the resources the country has rather than continue down an expensive and unsustainable road. His passion is for energy independence.

Pickens remains an outsized, polarizing character, but his empire was built on passion capital. He is now in the process of converting some of that to social capital. Pickens has taken the Giving Pledge, the decision to give most of his money to charitable causes. He has already given away $1 billion, including $500 million to Oklahoma State University, his alma mater.

When Passion Meets Politics: Squandering Resources

Passion can sometimes be killed by bureaucracies, or sacrificed by political expediency. It happened fifty years ago with psychiatric care. In the 1950s there were still what were euphemistically called madhouses all across North America. The major mental illnesses like schizophrenia and depression had no cure, and so thousands of people were housed in what were essentially warehouses for the mentally ill. And then in 1954 a major medical breakthrough was made by Montreal psychiatrist Heinz Lehmann.

Lehmann worked at the Douglas Hospital, which had 1600 patients and only four doctors on staff. In the medical literature, he had read of French scientists who were experimenting with a drug called chlorpromazine, which the government had hoped would cure sea-sickness in members of the armed forces deployed on troop ships. The drug didn't cure sea-sickness, but the scientists noted that it could be used to induce hypothermia. They began to experiment with it as a sedative.

Lehmann tried the drug on patients in the Douglas who had catatonia. The catatonics were silent and immobile, unresponsive to conversation, noise, or light. He made 16-millimetre films of himself talking to them. Some were so unresponsive that when he moved an arm into an odd position, it remained there, like a bent coat hanger.

But when he gave the patients chlorpromazine, they came out of their trances. It was, he said, like a miracle. They talked to him, told him they could hear him all this time but simply couldn't respond.

Lehmann knew he was onto something, and he was passionate about finding a cure for his patients. His workdays started at 8 a.m. and went past midnight. He continued to experiment with the drug, giving it to depressives and schizophrenics. Many of them showed a surprising response. He published his results in 1954 and was soon in contact with psychiatrists all over the world. This turned out to be both a good and a bad thing.

Lehmann was not only a scientist but also a clinician. He worked with patients every day. The drug had seemed like a miracle, but he knew it wasn't. It helped relieve symptoms but it didn't cure the patients, a critical difference. It was an important first step, but it wasn't the answer. The patients still needed treatment. They weren't ready to go back into society.

But that's what thousands of them did. Lehmann's research was seized upon by colleagues and then by American politicians as a "magic bullet." With one drug they thought they could cure the mentally ill. Not only that, they could empty the asylums and save money. For the U.S. government it was a win-win situation.

The process of deinstitutionalization that began in the United States in the 1960s saw the mentally ill treated with drugs, then released from institutions and left, in many cases, to fend for themselves.

It was a disaster. They didn't fit in. They couldn't cope in society. They were the precursors for what are now merely called "the homeless." Lehmann saw all this happen in his lifetime. He said that if he had it all to do over again, he might not have published his results. "It did just about as much bad as good," he said.

Lehmann had few resources. He had four hundred patients to care for, a sixteen-hour workday, no assistants, and no funding. But he was passionate about finding a way to help the mentally ill, and he was able to make a breakthrough. The government, with its vast resources, could have built on that. Instead, Lehmann's passion to help the mentally ill was railroaded by political expedience. His passion capital was undermined.

It isn't always the size of the resources that are available to us that determines success, but rather how those resources are used.

The Challenge of No Resources

In 1995, Craig Kielburger was a twelve-year-old student in Thornhill, Ontario, when he read a newspaper article about the death of another twelve-year-old boy halfway around the world. Iqbal Masih was a Pakistani boy who had worked as a slave in a carpet factory since he was four, chained to a loom, working fourteen-hour days. After he was freed by Pakistani police, Iqbal tried to bring the issue of child slavery into the open. He spoke to journalists and demonstrated. He was murdered as a result of this activism, and his murder was never solved.

Kielburger read more about child slavery and was surprised to find out how many children, many younger than himself, were kidnapped and used to make carpets or work with hazardous materials. He wanted to help these children, but they were on the other side of the world. He was twelve; he had no resources.

In school he asked for a show of hands of kids in his class who would help him. Eleven hands went up. Kielburger and his classmates formed an organization called Free The Children that was funded by garage sales, car washes, and bake sales run by Kielburger and his friends. They signed petitions and faxed them to the prime minister, Jean Chrétien, and other world leaders. Kielburger asked for a meeting with the prime minister and was turned down. So he called a press conference and said that Chrétien, who was travelling to India, had a moral responsibility to take action on the issue of child labour. Chrétien finally met with Kielburger and then brought up the issue of child labour with the trade delegation.

When he was fourteen, Kielburger raised enough money to go to South Asia and see some of these sweatshops first hand. Free The Children decided to focus its efforts on achievable goals. It lobbied to get Canada to label carpets, identifying those that weren't made by children, and to change the law so police could charge Canadians who hired child prostitutes in foreign countries.

Kielburger is now twenty-nine years old, and Free The Children has built more than five hundred schools and has projects in forty-five developing countries. The only resource he started with was the will of a suburban twelve-year-old. From that, an entire organization grew, one that has had an impact on thousands of lives in dozens of countries. We always have more resources than we think. Passion capital can grow from the smallest seed.

The Resource Curse

In a 1997 paper written for the Center for International Development and Harvard Institute for International Development, Jeffrey Sachs and Andrew Warner concluded that countries that were rich in resources tended to have poor economic growth. This paradox was labelled "the Resource Curse."

Their findings looked at the economic development of eighteen countries between 1970 and 1990. Among them, only two – Malaysia and Mauritius – showed economic growth, and that was only 2 per cent per annum. One of the reasons for this paradox was that the countries tended to concentrate on one resource, and as a result other industries either were undeveloped or became uncompetitive. Being a one-trick pony exposed them to fluctuations in commodity prices, which they couldn't control.

The existence of resources also gave countries a sense of wealth, and as a result, they borrowed against this wealth, the way homeowners started to use the equity in their homes like an ATM.

Sachs and Warner found that developing countries with abundant natural resources put less money into education than countries with few natural resources. They did so because there was little immediate need for it; locals could find high-paying semi-skilled jobs in the resource industries. Meanwhile, resource-poor countries such as Singapore, Korea, and Taiwan spent a lot on education. They had to compensate for their lack of natural resources. Their citizens would need to compete in knowledge industries.

Sometimes not having resources can be an advantage. People develop other assets to compensate for the absence of natural resources. Having a lot of resources can lull both countries and companies (and even individuals) into thinking they can coast. It can cause them to forget about creed, culture, and brand.

There are essentially two kinds of resources: renewable resources and non-renewable resources. Our behaviour often doesn't discriminate between the two. We act as though the non-renewables are endless. We are seeing this today with oil and at some point we will see it with water. In business we sometimes see it with money, the sense that you can always borrow more.

The way we identify, use, and preserve resources determines how our company will function. We can find resources in unexpected places, both within our companies and within ourselves.

KEY LESSONS

1. Resources are the assets that fuel growth and performance.

2. Resources can be financial, human, intellectual, or technological.

3. Passion capital flows when resources are allocated effectively, when the right resources are invested in the right place at the right time.

4. The size of available resources is not always related to the success achieved.

5. Resources, when marshalled and mastered, are the lifeblood of passion capital.

7

STRATEGY:

PLANNING WITH PASSION

Strategy without tactics is the slowest route to victory.
Tactics without strategy is the noise before defeat.
SUN TZU

Strategists are faced with the "one-year and five-year" paradox. Most people, companies, and countries overestimate
what they can achieve in a year, but underestimate what they
can achieve in five years. We jam too much into the first year,
because we want that measurable success; we can see that
horizon. The five-year horizon is too far away to properly focus
on. In many companies, it's viewed as the distant future. In
politics, it's light years away. The payoff is too far down the
road, and we tend to lose focus.

But this is what our focus should be on. In five years a
person can reinvent his career, a company can reinvent itself,
a country can chart a new course.

If you were to have fallen asleep in 1491 and woken up
in 1496, very little would have changed. And this despite a

momentous event: Columbus discovered America. But unless you were among the elite, you probably wouldn't have heard about it. There wasn't any mass media, and at any rate you would likely be illiterate. Even if you did hear about it, it wouldn't have had much impact on your life, unless you were a mapmaker. Your life would have been the same as your grandfather's, and your grandson's life would be similar to yours. But as change comes increasingly faster, it is difficult to see how new discoveries will affect us in the near future.

A 1949 issue of *Popular Mechanics* talked about the thirty-ton Electronic Numerical Integrator and Calculator, or ENIAC, computer and the amazing things it was capable of doing. The magazine predicted that in fifty years, we would have computers that weighed less than one and a half tons. No one could foresee a laptop that was thinner than a wallet and fifty thousand times faster than ENIAC.

Progress follows need, and the market defines need. In 1949, no one cared if computers were the size of bungalows. Only a handful of people even knew they existed. The idea that you could have one in your house didn't enter the consumer imagination for another three decades.

But it isn't just the consumer who has trouble grasping the future. Sometimes even the people who are *creating* the future don't realize what they have. In a *New Yorker* article titled "Creation Myth," Malcolm Gladwell recounted how Steve Jobs got the essential ideas for what would become the first Macintosh computer. In 1979, Jobs was a twenty-four-year-old tech entrepreneur. He had already started Apple, and it had generated some buzz in Silicon Valley. But the reigning tech powerhouse at the time was Xerox PARC, which was the innovation arm of Xerox. Jobs offered Xerox a deal. They could buy 100,000 shares of Apple for $1 million when the IPO was floated the following year if they would show him what they were working on.

Xerox took the offer and gave Jobs a tour. He ended up in front of the Xerox Alto, the personal computer that PARC was working on. It had a "mouse" which Jobs had never seen. And instead of typing in instructions, which was standard then for computers, it had icons that you just clicked on. You could open and close "windows." Jobs shouted, "Why aren't you doing anything with this? This is the greatest thing. This is revolutionary!"

But Xerox didn't do anything with it. Little more than a year later they withdrew from the personal computer market. Jobs went back to Apple and worked on his own mouse, on icons, on windows. The result was the Macintosh, the computer that revolutionized the personal computer market.

Years later, Jobs said, "If Xerox had known what it had and had taken advantage of its real opportunities it could have been as big as IBM plus Microsoft plus Xerox combined – and the largest high-technology company in the world."

Instead Xerox fell far behind the pack. Even though it held the future in its hands, it wasn't able to see it. The innovations were brilliant, but the strategy failed. Without strategy, both passion and innovation are left stranded, to be picked up by someone else.

Freedom 55. Or 65. Or 95.

In 1984, insurance company London Life began airing adver-
tisements with the catchphrase "Freedom 55." The phrase is
still part of the language, but whatever promise it held almost
thirty years ago is pretty much gone. The idea of retiring ten
years before what has become the standard retirement age –
sixty-five – was attractive, but it never became a reality for
most people.

The main reason for this is lack of planning.

An Environics poll conducted for TD Waterhouse asked
people between the ages of forty-five and sixty-four about
their retirement. Thirty-two per cent said they planned to win
a lottery to finance their retirement. An almost equal number
– 34 per cent – said they had money saved for retirement. The
remaining 34 per cent were somewhere between these two
positions. An Ipsos Reid poll done for Standard Life showed
that 44 per cent of people with group retirement plans didn't
know what their income would be in retirement. Thirty-eight
per cent said they would continue to work past retirement age
out of financial necessity.

Retirement is something that many people are passionate
about. They visualize relaxing on a beach or on their porch,
or travelling to exotic places. They count the days before they
can leave their job and relax. Yet their energy often goes
toward how the time is spent, not on how to pay for it. It's passion without planning.

Some of the people interviewed by TD Waterhouse were
sixty-four years old and hoping to retire in a year or less. It is
unsettling that a third of them were counting on winning a

lottery in the next twelve months. But it speaks to our relationship with the future. Many people don't want the hard realities of their financial situation to interfere with the seductive fantasies of their retirement. Few people want to embrace bad news until they have to.

Most individuals don't have a plan for their retirement or even for their career. But most companies have some kind of strategic plan. They are called by different names: environmental scans, strengths-weaknesses-opportunities-threats (SWOT) analysis, and so on. Alas, most of these fail.

One of the reasons these strategies fail is that their planning is based on a future that looks a lot like the present. Another reason is that they don't look far enough ahead. Most passion capitalists plan for the long term. It isn't an easy thing to do, but the first step is to grasp the fundamental nature of your business.

Look at the example of Blockbuster Video. CEO Wayne Huizinga, realizing the potential of the home video market, bought controlling interest in the company in the 1980s and built it into North America's largest video store chain. In 1994 Blockbuster was sold to Viacom for $8.4 billion; Viacom turned around and sold it to Wherehouse Entertainment in 1998, who were themselves bought by Trans World Entertainment.

This corporate version of hot potato was underpinned by the fact that the way people were getting their video entertainment was changing. In February 2009, Blockbuster was listed first on *U.S. News and World Report*'s "15 Companies That Might Not Survive 2009." They weren't far off with their prediction. By May 2010, Blockbuster was the only national video chain left in the United States. That September, it too filed for bankruptcy, with debts of $900 million. Its losses were attributed directly to the advent of video-on-demand and companies like Netflix.

But the first video-on-demand experiments were carried out more than twenty years before, in wired communities that had access to early technologies. The early warnings were there when Huizinga bought Blockbuster in the 1980s.

Blockbuster has since been revived, and the new incarnation has a video-on-demand component. But the company's ultimate failure was that they didn't understand the competition and they didn't have a grasp of their market. They failed to create an effective strategy.

In every era, there are businesses that can see the world shifting away from them. They know their product has limited value in the near future, but like the frog in the slowly heating water, they don't get out before it boils.

The Evolution of Strategy

In the late nineteenth century, the buzzword in the corporate world was "science." Frederick Winslow Taylor (1856–1915), who has been called the father of the scientific management and efficiency movement, sought strategies to improve efficiency in both offices and factories. His weapon was science, or perhaps more accurately "science." He had a Presbyterian idea that waste was a sin, and he was passionate about making the American workplace more efficient. He advocated the scientific study of every task, no matter how simple or mundane.

Then every employee could be scientifically trained to perform his or her task.

One of Taylor's underlying assumptions was that there was a science to almost everything. "I can say, without the slightest hesitation," he told a congressional committee, "that the science of handling pig-iron is so great that the man who is physically able to handle pig-iron and is sufficiently phlegmatic and stupid to choose this for his occupation is rarely able to comprehend the science of handling pig-iron."

At the time, the world was in the throes of the machine age, and the goal was to have people, as far as possible, mimic machines. Taylor also engaged in a now familiar tactic – make everything seem more complicated than it is so you need to hire a consultant to come in and set things right. There isn't a science to handling pig-iron, but "science" was to the last century what "brand" is to this one. Taylor implemented "time and motion studies," and his theories continued to evolve through the early part of the twentieth century and took root in corporate America. One person Taylor influenced was Charles Bedaux. Bedaux was born in Paris, dropped out of school in 1903, and learned street-fighting and dressing for success from a pimp named Ledoux, who was eventually murdered. Bedaux subsequently moved to America, and after working at several largely unrelated jobs, started a scientific management business in Cleveland.

Bedaux became a millionaire by selling management strategies. By the 1930s, more than five hundred American companies were using his system, including General Electric, Standard Oil, and Eastman Kodak. His methods dominated the British workplace and were sold in twenty-one countries.

Bedaux didn't do much to expand on Taylor's ideas; what he did was find a way to market the techniques. Efficiency is a new science, he declared. Bedaux was a gifted salesman, and he was able to sell both science and increased profits.

One of Bedaux's improvements on Taylor's efficiency systems was to establish a way to measure results. Bedaux argued that all human labour could be measured in definite units of effort and fatigue, and he modestly named them Bedaux units. These were based on the "principle of human power measurement." He aimed for 80 BUs per hour. Who knows if any of those companies benefited from Bedaux's theories. But Bedaux certainly did.

Bedaux had a passion for life. He liked women and champagne and parties. He bought a chateau in France, and that was where the Duke of Windsor and Wallis Simpson were married after Edward abdicated the throne of England. Bedaux also had a genuine passion for efficiency and an effective strategy for getting his message out, for literally changing the corporate world.

But despite devoting his life to corporate and management strategy, Bedaux's strategies for his own life were less impressive. In 1934, he led an expedition grandly named the Bedaux Canadian Sub-Arctic Expedition. It started from Edmonton, Alberta, and was supposed to go fifteen hundred miles through northern British Columbia to Telegraph Creek. Fitness training was scheduled in the town of Jasper, but the crew didn't actually do any training and instead attended champagne parties in their honour. Bedaux left Edmonton in July, accompanied by his wife, his mistress, a cinematographer, guides, surveyors, twenty cowboys, a hundred horses, cooks, a valet, and a maid. The party also took along five newly developed Citroën half-track vehicles. The expedition wasn't a success. Two of the vehicles fell off a cliff, one drifted down a river, and the other two were abandoned when it was clear they were no use in the swampy territory. The party ran short of supplies, Bedaux's wife and mistress didn't get along, and the expedition came to a halt short of its goal.

Bedaux's strategy for his expedition lacked a number of things, chiefly a realistic sense of the weather and terrain he would be dealing with. And the somewhat French concept of taking along both your wife and mistress (who was an Italian countess) seems a dangerous strategy. He packed a tuxedo, a bathtub, caviar, and several cases of champagne. It was a very expensive, incredibly inefficient trip. It was odd that Bedaux wasn't able to adapt any of his own strategies to his expedition.

It is sometimes easier to see the faults of others than to see our own inefficiencies, but understanding ourselves is key to formulating an effective strategy. Passion capital is based on creed, and creeds should be rooted in self-knowledge.

Strategies evolve because the culture evolves, corporations evolve, and workers evolve. Every era throws out a new buzzword, a new corporate strategy that is based on science, or the code of the samurai, or Winnie the Pooh. But strategies need to contain an element of common sense. It was the lack of common sense in a St. Louis factory where Bedaux had once worked that got him interested in efficiency in the first place. But he ultimately lacked common sense when planning for himself. He committed suicide in a Miami prison cell in 1944 after being accused of going into business with the Nazis during wartime – another ill-conceived strategy.

Those early strategies devised by Taylor and Bedaux were an attempt to institutionalize efficiency. They were supposed to work everywhere, whether an insurance office, a steel mill, or a warehouse in New Jersey. Perhaps they did. What makes a workplace efficient isn't always obvious. In a study that appears in Thomas Peters and Robert Waterman's seminal work *In Search of Excellence*, it was noted that turning the lights up in a factory increased efficiency. Interestingly, when they were later turned down again, efficiency increased yet again. Peters and Waterman concluded that it wasn't the levels of light that had any effect on the workers, but the simple fact that management was paying attention to them. The workers responded to the attention, not to the light levels.

At the time they published their book, in 1982, Peters and Waterman worked for McKinsey & Company, a management consulting firm. Founded in Chicago in 1926, McKinsey has grown into a global corporation that employs nine thousand consultants in fifty-six countries. One of its past managing directors, Marvin Bower (1950–67), is considered the father of modern management consulting, the logical heir to the efficiency movement started by Taylor.

The current managing director of McKinsey is Dominic Barton, who has argued that passion is critical to business and critical to McKinsey. "Passion is key," he says. "You don't always have to be logical. Don't do something because of what you think it might get you, do it because you're passionate about it." He has argued that business has a noble purpose. "I very much believe this," he said. "Milton Friedman was full of crap on that point; that business is business and it will take care of everything. We have to ask ourselves what we can do to make the earth a better place."

One of the obstacles to that goal is the rampant short-term strategies that have infected western capitalism. Barton wrote an article in the *Harvard Business Review* titled "Capitalism for the Long Term," in which he argued that the emphasis on quarterly earnings was crippling businesses in the West. "It's like planting an apple tree and pulling it out by the roots every three months to see how it's doing," he says. In the East, they are looking at the long term. South Korean president Lee Myung-bak asked Barton to help formulate a sixty-year plan for that country. China's policies are geared toward fifty to a hundred years.

Barton advocates a form of passion capitalism – the need to start with a creed, to be infused with passion, to go against shareholders in the short term in order to benefit all stakeholders in the longer term. He cited the example of the iPod. When it was released in 2001, it sold only 400,000 units, and Apple's share price dropped by roughly 25 per cent. Eight years later, the iPod had sold 220 million units and revolutionized the music industry. Apple shares were up, and the company was on its way to becoming the largest corporation on earth.

According to McKinsey studies, building a profitable business takes between five and seven years. But the market is impatient. It can't wait that long for a business to be profitable, and it doesn't wait long for existing businesses to realize their goals. The average time frame that investors held a single stock used to be seven years; today it's closer to seven months. The ADD generation is creating a short-term world whose short-term strategies are killing innovation and productivity – and almost killed capitalism itself.

It takes courage to create a strategy that might scare shareholders in the short term but benefit all stakeholders in the longer term. In his role with McKinsey, Barton helps create those strategies. His own story has been one of persistence. He was one of only six people in his high school to go to university. At McKinsey, he was up for partner three times before making it. The company has an "up or out" policy that means people who apply for senior positions advance or they go elsewhere. But Barton's persistence paid off: he was made partner, then global managing director.

From that vantage point, he oversees strategies for companies, non-profit organizations, and governments. McKinsey's counsel is to look to the long term and to the big picture: to look beyond the needs of shareholders to the needs of all stakeholders – employees, suppliers, customers, creditors, communities, and the environment. These needs aren't at odds with maximizing corporate value, Barton argues. In fact, they are essential to that goal. These are the principles of passion capitalism, and the most viable strategy for a sustainable and profitable future.

Here are the four steps to building a strategy that helps us create passion capital:

1. START WITH CREED

Your creed is the starting point and touchstone for developing a great strategy. The right creed sets forth the fundamental beliefs, ambition, and long-term purpose found at the starting point of great strategies. Belief, purpose, and ambition are the bedrock of strategic plans that build passion capital.

2. REPLACE SWOT WITH SPOT

Most strategic plans use some form of SWOT (Strengths, Weaknesses, Opportunities, and Threats) analysis. An important change needs to be made here. "Passion" needs to replace "Weaknesses." So, the right analytics should focus on Strengths, Passion, Opportunities, and Threats, or SPOT. In developing strategy for the future, the greatest emphasis should be in examining strengths and passion. So, think SPOT, not SWOT.

3. DEFINE SUCCESS

"What is success?" is another of those simple questions that is often difficult to answer. Yet every career, company, and cause should have a clear answer to this question. So much time and attention is wasted in strategic planning, yet this direct and simple question goes unanswered. Every great strategic plan should outline exactly what success looks like in specific and measurable terms.

4. CREATE A JOB JAR

Strategy has become more complicated and sophisticated, but not more effective or efficient. Starting with a strong creed statement, doing SPOT analysis, and defining what success looks like leads to a natural fourth step. A colleague I worked with, Ray Verdun, was an excellent CEO (formerly with Nabisco Brands in Canada and the U.S.). Ray used to ask people, "What's in your job jar?" Most companies have endless objectives, strategies, tactics, projects, and plans. The job jar is both a practical and symbolic way to prioritize. I have a job jar that sits on my desk and has only one piece of paper in it. It's dated November 9, 2011, and reads, "Go raise $1 billion over five years for Personalized Cancer Medicine at Princess Margaret." It's a constant reminder that a complex strategy has been built around a single job. Everyone in the organization should have a job jar, and everyone's job jar should be transparent and accessible to others in the organization.

Emerging Strategies

Sunil Mittal's path to becoming a telecom billionaire was strewn with obstacles, though he always felt he would get there. "Even while in school I aspired to achieve great things in life," Mittal told *The Times of India*. "Admittedly, I wasn't quite sure about what these great things would be."

He started his first business, a venture that traded bicycle parts and hosiery yarn, at the age of eighteen, using $450 borrowed from his father. The business was marginal and involved extensive travel, and Mittal didn't have money for plane tickets. He travelled in the backs of trucks with his goods, stayed in hostels, and worked sixteen-hour days. Yet he remained optimistic despite the discouraging numbers and gruelling schedule.

In 1981, at the age of twenty-four, he started importing Suzuki portable generators from Japan and became one of

India's largest importers of gensets. Two years later the famously corrupt Indian government (it would be thirty years before mass protests erupted against this entrenched corruption) dictated that the import of generators was banned. Mittal was out of business overnight.

Two years later he was importing push-button phones, which he'd seen in Taiwan. India was still using rotary phones. Mittal started marketing phones and fax machines, and in 1992, he won a bid for one of the four mobile phone licences that were auctioned in India. In 1995, his company Bharti Cellular was formed. Not one to sit still for long, Mittal recognized the growing middle class in India and entered a joint venture deal with Wal-Mart to build stores in his country.

Mittal built an empire on phones. He understood that in a country that has little infrastructure, wireless communication was going to be big.

"One should sense opportunity at the beginning of a curve," Mittal said, "and venture into hitherto unexplored fields." He has also said, "There will be difficulties on the way – but everything in life is possible."

Office Strategies of the Future

Can you run a business using just a phone? Could you run a business without any of the standard support mechanisms? What if you didn't have an assistant, or a sales force, or management, or labour? Or even an office? Can you run a business where your only tool is a cell phone?

The firm tinePublic, which books public speakers (mostly

former politicians), does just that. TinePublic has two partners – Andy McCreath and Christian Darbyshire – and no
office or employees, an efficiency that would surely surprise
even Charles Bedaux.

McCreath and Darbyshire started their business in 2002
with a question: How do we get the former president of the
United States to do a speaking tour? If you are an established
speaker's agency offering large fees, it isn't that difficult. But
for two guys in their late twenties who live in Calgary and had
no track record, it's another story. What is the strategy to realize their goal?

McCreath had briefly worked for the National Hockey
League office in New York, and Darbyshire had sold mutual
funds and photocopiers. Neither of them had any experience
on the lecture circuit. Bill Clinton had been out of office for
two years when they first called his people to see about a
speaking tour. The answer, unsurprisingly, was no.

McCreath and Darbyshire realized they needed some kind
of track record. And so they put on an event called the Young
Professionals and Entrepreneurs Conference, in Calgary, their
first show. The main draw was Bill Rancic, who had recently
been the winner on Donald Trump's show *The Apprentice*.
The conference drew two thousand people. They did three
more Young Professionals events. Now they had a track record
of sorts, though it wasn't in exactly the same area. They continued their regular calls to Clinton's people.

Clinton finally acquiesced. The first engagement, in
London, Ontario, in 2005, drew six thousand people, and
McCreath and Darbyshire ended up doing eight more events
with Clinton. They were the first to get George Bush when

he left office and did five events with him. And in an illustration of the old saying that politics makes strange bedfellows, they did one event with both Bush and Clinton together. They also booked Rudy Giuliani and Tony Blair, and got Gene Simmons of Kiss to talk about marketing to a group of young entrepreneurs in Saskatoon.

When they booked Alan Greenspan after he'd stepped down as chairman of the Federal Reserve, he was supposed to appear in the ballroom of Toronto's Sheraton Hotel. Unfortunately, the Washington airport was snowed in and Greenspan couldn't get there. Two thousand Toronto CEOs who had paid $400 to see him speak milled about unhappily. Darbyshire and McCreath finally rigged up a video link and got Greenspan into a Washington studio. His mournful face appeared on a large screen at the front of the ballroom. It was late, and he wasn't there in person, but the two entrepreneurs had saved the event with their resourcefulness. They fully anticipated having to refund much of the money they'd taken in, but not one of the CEOs asked for their money back.

One thing they quickly discovered was that politicians, no matter how big, aren't rock stars. Their initial strategy was to sell tickets to their events through Ticketmaster. When George Bush was booked for Calgary, only 120 advance tickets were sold through Ticketmaster. It was a shock that the former president, out of office for less than a year, would draw roughly what a poetry reading does in conservative, oil-mad Calgary, a natural constituency for him. Ads in the papers didn't help that much either. Of the 1800 tickets eventually sold for the Bush event, 1400 were sold directly by McCreath and Darbyshire over the phone to corporations.

Both McCreath and Darbyshire have full decision-making power, so "the office" is wherever they happen to be. They are in constant communication, both with clients and with each other. The cell phone is their data collector, their life-line, their only key tool. This was their office strategy.

Because at least one of the partners needed to be at every event, and the events were sometimes clustered (there were three Bush events on three consecutive nights in different cities), McCreath and Darbyshire were on the road a lot of the time. The no-office, no-employee model gave them efficiency, flexibility, and immediacy. They solved each problem as it came up. They were the beginnings of a new corporate strategy: BlackBerry Nation.

There are dozens of corporate and management strategies out there. But sometimes it can be useful to return to first principles. What does your company really need? Instead of tailoring an existing strategy to your business, you may benefit from a revolutionary strategy of your own devising.

Passionate Strategy

Harlequin Romances have become synonymous with romance novels, an enviable thing for any brand. Since the company was established more than sixty years ago, it has shipped almost six billion books.

Writing all those books is an army of people who follow strict guidelines regarding length, tone, character, and theme. These guidelines are available online, and thousands of people try their hand at writing a Harlequin novel, hoping for spectacular mass market success and easy money. Harlequin receives more than a thousand manuscripts a month. If you read one or two of the books, you can see why so many people think they could write one. They are short and formulaic, and the writing is rudimentary at best.

Yet few people succeed at the genre. The ones who do tend to be the true believers. The grad student who sees it as a way to make a quick buck is soon disillusioned. Many of the books are written by former readers who fell in love with the genre. It turns out you need to have a passion for passion, even if it is formulaic.

The company was founded on the idea of romance, but what set Harlequin apart was its strategy. It was started in Winnipeg in 1949 by Richard Bonnycastle, a lawyer and, oddly, a former fur trader for the Hudson's Bay Company. Initially, Harlequin reprinted British and American paperbacks of all kinds for the Canadian market, until in 1957 it became the North American distributor for Mills & Boon, a British publisher of romances. It turned out to be the most lucrative genre.

The turning point came in 1971, when Bonnycastle bought Mills & Boon and named W. Lawrence Heisey president of Harlequin. Heisey had an MBA from Harvard and was coming from Procter & Gamble, where he described himself, self-deprecatingly, as a "soap salesman." His passion was marketing, and in the P&G world, it was critical. It wasn't critical in the book world, however, which has long existed largely outside of any traditional marketing paradigm.

What Heisey did was adapt the marketing strategies of the consumer product world to the notoriously unstrategic book world. He started by doing market research on romance readers. Who were they? How old? How busy? He found out that young and middle-aged women were the primary readers.

Once he had identified his customers, Heisey found innovative ways to reach them. He put the books in supermarkets, because that's where these women were several times a week. He made the Harlequin name larger on the books to promote brand awareness. He advertised on daytime television, an unheard-of strategy in the book business, and at one point included sample romances in boxes of Bio-Ad detergent.

He also started a subscription service that targeted rural readers who weren't near a bookstore or supermarket, but urban readers also bought into the service. The subscription service accomplished several things. It expanded the market. It also eliminated the expense of retailers and returns (bookstores return unsold books to publishers, and publishers pay both for the return shipping and, eventually, for pulping the unsold books). And it also gave Heisey precise data on who his consumer was.

Heisey moved the company into the American market, and his success there quickly spawned competition. Dell started its Candlelight Ecstasy series, and Simon and Schuster launched Silhouette, which took Heisey's marketing ideas even further and test-marketed manuscripts on target readers.

The romance market, which had always existed, was awakened with, well, a passion. In 1981, Torstar, the company that owns the *Toronto Star* and already had a stake in Harlequin, bought controlling shares. It then began buying up Harlequin's competitors, including Silhouette.

Essentially, the Harlequin line is reader-driven. As the readers became more diverse, so did the books. There are several lines today, ranging from religious romances (no kissing) to the Wedlocked! series (marriage) to what is essentially erotica. The strategy has made Harlequin the dominant publisher of romance novels in the world. In the fourth quarter of 2008, Torstar, along with most companies, suffered losses. But romance conquers all: Harlequin's profits rose by 11.2 per cent.

By adapting consumer product strategies to the book business, Heisey was able to go after the market with an efficiency that other publishers lacked. He had an advantage in that he had a homogeneous product: he was selling passion (or at least a facsimile of it). Heisey's strategy was based on the understanding that Harlequin books had more in common with laundry detergent than they did with literary fiction. Heisey realized that Harlequin, despite appearances, is only nominally in the book business. It was selling a product – romantic escape. Harlequin may be the most literal example of turning passion into passion capital.

Lessons of War:
Is My Strategy Right or Is Everyone Else Wrong?

Casey Stengel, the colourful, oft-quoted manager of the New York Yankees and New York Mets baseball teams, said, "Most games are lost, not won." The same has been said of wars. The battle on the Plains of Abraham in 1759 between the French commander, the Marquis de Montcalm, and the British brigadier-general James Wolfe could fall into that category. It has been billed as the Battle for a Continent. In those pre–American Revolution days, North America was still up for grabs. In terms of pure real estate, the Plains of Abraham was probably the biggest battle in history.

It was won by the daring of General Wolfe, or so most history books tell us. But was it Wolfe's strategic genius that won the day?

Let's look at the circumstances. Wolfe left England with a quarter of the British navy – fifteen thousand men in 186 ships. The fleet stretched for a hundred miles up the St. Lawrence River when it arrived in June. But when Wolfe got to Quebec City and saw that heavily walled fortress high above steep cliffs, he despaired. He had all those resources but no strategy. He didn't know what to do. He made one ill-conceived try at landing upriver, and his men were cut down by fire from above.

Then he sat in his ship's cabin and fretted. The summer went by. Wolfe was in poor health and filled with indecision; he was ridiculed by his men. He would have to turn around before the end of September to winter in Britain or risk getting iced in on the river and starving to death. The humiliation of returning without even having engaged the enemy, especially with this massive force, would kill his career. So in early September he hatched a plan out of desperation. His plan was to climb a goat path that wound up an undefended four-hundred-foot-high cliff, and to do so in the dead of night.

On the night of September 12, Wolfe's men reluctantly made the climb, and then overwhelmed the few sentries at the top. When Montcalm awoke that morning it was to find five hundred British soldiers sitting outside the fortress of Quebec. Montcalm had three thousand troops that were only a three-hour march away. He could have waited. The British would have been hard pressed to storm the fortress. But he didn't wait. He came out with his tired army and faced the British on the Plains. The battle was over in a matter of minutes. The continent was won. Wolfe was a genius.

Or was he? He'd acted out of desperation, and then Montcalm made a critical tactical error that gave the British their victory. Wolfe died in the battle, so we can't say whether he would have distinguished himself as a military figure had he lived. His epic victory could have been a one-off. Certainly his officers were worried about his competence and indecisiveness and wrote about it in their journals. When Wolfe's body was put into a barrel of rum to preserve it for the trip back to England, the men complained that it was a waste of good rum. Even in victory he was unloved.

We see similar situations in business when a CEO catches the right market conditions or benefits from the mistakes of a competitor and then thinks he's a genius. But it isn't his strategy that won the day. It was the failed strategies of others or an unforeseen event. It's important to review your strategies even when they're successful. They may not have been successful for the reasons you thought they were.

People are undone by their success almost as often as their failures. The reason is not understanding the success, not knowing how it was achieved, and then not realizing how to sustain it.

You can be lucky in battle a few times, but over the long term, that luck won't hold. You need to be clear about which strategies are working and *why* they are working. Strategy in business depends on three issues: know yourself, know the enemy, know the market.

Passion can be squandered through a poor strategy, but at least everyone knows what went wrong. A poor strategy that's successful makes a shaky foundation for passion capital, because no one understands why it went right.

It's Only Rock and Roll (or Is It?)

Rock and roll music has always been a potent force for change. But it never had a strategy. Its raw power changed the culture, but that wasn't according to anyone's plan (despite early parental protests that the devil was behind it). But what if you attached a plan to it?

In 1984, Bob Geldof, singer and songwriter for the Irish band the Boomtown Rats, saw a BBC news report on the devastating famine in Ethiopia. With fellow rock artist Midge Ure, he wrote "Do They Know It's Christmas?" to raise money for famine relief. He was able to appeal to British rock royalty to record the song, which appeared under the name Band Aid, and featured vocals by Sting, Phil Collins, Bono, and George Michael, among others. The single sold three million copies in its first week, the fastest-selling single in British history (a record it held for thirteen years), and raised more than $15 million for famine relief.

With the success of that single, Geldof realized that the extraordinary power – both cultural and financial – of rock and roll could be steered toward philanthropy. If managed properly, it could raise both money and awareness. He and Ure then organized Live Aid, which was staged simultaneously at Wembley Stadium in London and JFK Stadium in

Philadelphia. The BBC cleared the airwaves for sixteen hours to broadcast live in the U.K. Live Aid raised more than $140 million for famine relief. The irreverent thirty-four-year-old Geldof (who at one point in the live broadcast yelled, "Give us your fucking money!") was subsequently knighted.

On a visit to Africa in 2004, Geldof realized that the threat of starvation was still dire. He talked to British prime minister Tony Blair, who then commissioned a study. The seventeen commissioners given the task of studying Africa's problems included Geldof and various African politicians. They delivered their recommendations (debt relief, a doubling of foreign aid, trade reform) a year later, but the G8 leaders showed little interest.

So Geldof pursued the same strategy he'd used for Live Aid. This time he staged eight simultaneous concerts, in each of the G8 countries, in the week before the G8 Summit. The event was titled Live 8 and it was intended to bring attention to the issue and to put pressure on European politicians. Staged in iconic venues (Hyde Park in London, Versailles in France, Red Square in Moscow), Live 8 was ambitious in both scale and conception. The logistics were confounding: more than a thousand musicians performed, and the performances were broadcast on 182 TV networks and two thousand radio stations. Live 8 claimed a viewership/listenership of three billion people.

Geldof grasped that the massive (though admittedly diffuse and chaotic) power of rock and roll could be steered toward specific targets. To use it effectively involved a staggering logistics problem, but he had a strategy that was made for a specific outcome. The timing, the iconic venues, the blanket coverage – it was all designed to get the issues of African starvation and poverty on the table at the Summit. It worked. The G8 leaders used the commission's recommendations for African debt and aid reform.

Rock and roll was always Geldof's passion, but with Live 8, he found a way to turn it into passion capital. The music that had inspired his youth and had given him his career was now being used to deal with hunger and poverty in Africa.

KEY LESSONS

1. Strategy is a plan to achieve a specific goal. Strategy is the brain of passion capital.

2. Most strategies overestimate what can be accomplished in a year and underestimate what can be accomplished in five years.

3. The typical strategic planning tool of SWOT analysis (Strengths, Weaknesses, Opportunities, Threats) needs to be replaced by SPOT analysis (Strengths, Passion, Opportunities, Threats).

4. Passion is a critical component of effective strategic planning.

5. Strategy needs to have a much longer time horizon than next quarter or next year.

8

PERSISTENCE:

IF AT FIRST YOU DON'T SUCCEED

Money grows on the tree of persistence.
JAPANESE PROVERB

All breakthroughs in cancer research are the result of persistence, whether it's individual or institutional persistence. It's a quality that I admire and one that is necessary to the work at Princess Margaret Hospital. It's a quality that was celebrated at the TEDMED conference – an annual conference that deals with the future of healthcare and medicine – in San Diego in 2009. I went with my colleague and friend Dr. Shaf Keshavjee, a lung transplant specialist, who was a keynote speaker. Shaf pioneered a technology that keeps lungs alive outside the body. I was there to learn and to help Shaf demonstrate this technology.

Before Shaf spoke, an opera singer named Charity Tillerman-Dick sang an aria. What made her performance so moving was the fact that she had had a double lung transplant a year earlier. She had been told she would never sing again, but here she was, her voice as powerful as ever. The audience was moved to tears by her story and her performance.

Shaf got up to speak after the ovation and told the story of lung transplants. They were pioneered in Toronto in the early 1980s, but Shaf and his team had taken them to a new level. Five minutes into his talk, I pushed onto the stage a special chamber the size of a grocery cart. Inside was a living, breathing pig's lung. There were gasps from the audience. Before the session, I had spoken to Martha Stewart, who was in the audience. I asked her if she'd come onstage, slip on surgical gloves, and hold the lung in her hands. She gamely agreed, and she and Shaf brought the house down.

There was a dinner on the beach that night, and Shaf and I chatted with Jay Walker, the entrepreneur who had come up with Priceline.com, which allows consumers to name their own price when looking for airline tickets. Walker used some of the money he made from Priceline and other ventures to amass one of the largest private libraries in the world. Among his extraordinary collection are some of the earliest known medical textbooks. At TEDMED, he showed us what is generally agreed to be the first medical textbook, along with other medical books he had bought, including a rare 1496 Renaissance tome.

Walker's interest in both medical matters and entrepreneurial issues dovetailed at TEDMED, and he bought the conference in 2011. In listening to his presentation and talking to him on the beach, I became increasingly interested in Walker's remarkable story. He is a passion capitalist, and he is an illuminating study in persistence, one of those people who has faced many hurdles but keeps trying, regardless of how many and how high they are.

His hero, unsurprisingly, is Thomas Edison, who was also famously persistent. When Edison was working on a way to commercialize the light bulb and failed 9,999 times in the attempt, a reporter asked if he was going to fail 10,000 times. "I have not failed at each attempt," Edison replied. "Rather, I've succeeded at discovering another way not to invent the electric lamp." As a scientist he was aware that his next experiment could be the one that is successful. "Many of life's failures," he said, "are people who did not realize how close they were to success when they gave up." Edison failed systematically – each failed experiment brought him closer to success.

Jay Walker holds more than two hundred patents (one of only a dozen living inventors to do so – Edison held a thousand), but is known chiefly for founding Priceline.com. But Priceline wasn't Walker's first business venture. After dropping out of Cornell University, he started a free weekly paper in Ithaca, New York. It did well until the local daily paper – which was run by the mighty Gannett Corporation, the largest newspaper publisher in the United States – brought out its own free weekly and put Walker out of business. He went back to Cornell and graduated, albeit with $150,000 worth of debt from his failed newspaper venture.

He then moved to New York City and started a company called Visual Technologies, which sold interactive glass sculptures. The sculptures flashed electromagnetic light when touched. But they were too expensive for the market, and Visual Technologies filed for bankruptcy in 1986. This time Walker owed $5.3 million.

After that, Walker ran Catalog Media, a corporation that tried to sell ad space in catalogues and then sell the catalogues in bookstores. By 1988, it too was gone. The next venture was NewSub Services, which sold magazine subscriptions through credit card companies. It wasn't until 1995 that Walker founded Walker Digital. One focus of this new company was how things were sold. Walker had been circling that idea with his other ventures, but with Walker Digital it started to take flight. It was out of this thinking that Priceline was born.

Walker's central idea was that certain products had a shelf life. An unsold airline seat had no value after take-off; an unsold hotel room had no value after midnight. Would companies agree to sell some of their unused and highly perishable inventory at a reduced price to people who were making last-minute travel arrangements?

In 1998, Walker received the patent for his consumer-driven model; it was the first time the U.S. Patent Office had granted a patent for a business method. His concept essentially turned the consumer/provider relationship on its head. Rather than comparing prices offered by competing companies, the consumer put out her desired price and waited to see who would respond.

Priceline wasn't an instant hit. In its first year, only 7 per cent of bidders got an airline seat, not a brilliant record. And the company lost $30 on every ticket it sold. In 1999, Walker took Priceline public. Two days after the IPO, his shares were worth $5.2 billion. A year later the stock had gone from $162 to $3, a victim of the tech crash, and Walker sold his Priceline shares to Hong Kong investors.

He returned to Walker Digital and continued to patent business models. In 2003, he approached the U.S. government with an Internet-based security company, called U.S. HomeGuard, that proposed putting 47,000 cameras around vulnerable sites such as airports, nuclear facilities, and water reservoirs. The idea was that the government would pay people to watch the images from their homes and report suspicious activity.

When this idea didn't fly, he looked to using smart technology on vending machines and gambling systems. And in 2009, he launched a free website that helps non-English-speakers learn the language.

Walker's passion for innovation led to him establish the Walker Library of the History of Human Imagination, a fifty-thousand-item library that contains a 1250 edition of the Bible written on sheepskin; an illustrated medical book from the fifteenth century; a 1699 atlas – the first to put the sun at the centre of the universe; the napkin on which Franklin Roosevelt sketched his plan to win World War II; and an original 1957 *Sputnik* satellite. He has both a sixteenth-century map that is the first to show North and South America and the map that astronauts took to the Moon. "If this can happen in five hundred years," he has said of the two maps, "nothing is impossible."

The human imagination is at the root of all innovation, of all progress, but it was persistence as much as innovation that accounted for Walker's success. As his hero Thomas Edison famously said, "Genius is 10 per cent inspiration and 90 per cent perspiration."

Emerging Persistence

The insurance business goes back to 2100 B.C. in Babylonia, when traders wanted guarantees for the safe arrival of their goods. The Greeks and Phoenicians later adopted something similar for their ships. The Romans were the first to provide burial insurance. The first extant insurance contract was signed in Genoa, in 1347, and the practice quickly became entrenched. Policies were signed by people who stipulated the amount of risk they were willing to assume for outgoing ships. The term "underwriter" stems from those first policies.

In 1688, the first insurance company was formed, in Lloyd's Coffee House in London, where shipowners, merchants, and underwriters often met to discuss business. Lloyd's of London went on to become synonymous with insurance. Five years later, the astronomer Edmond Halley developed the first mortality table, and the life insurance industry was born.

These practices gradually spread through much of the world, and our risk was mitigated. We now had some protection against disease, floods, piracy, drunk drivers. One of the few global holdouts, though, was China.

Historically, the Chinese have been great savers. That is how they deal with risk. When faced with the concept of insurance, they embraced the idea of pension and medical benefits, but found the idea of death benefits too morbid to contemplate, let alone pay for. This essential cultural difference made it difficult for life insurance to get much traction in China.

In 1988, Peter Ma, a thirty-one-year-old Chinese government official, convinced local governments that they would need car insurance in the Special Economic Zone (SEZ) that was being created by Deng Xiaoping. At the time, the city of Shenzhen, the centre of the SEZ, was still essentially a fishing village. The idea of car insurance was alien. For one thing, there were hardly any cars. Today Shenzhen has 12 million people and epic traffic that makes Los Angeles look rural in comparison. On the twelve-lane freeways that course through the city, it isn't unusual to see transport trucks, European cars, tiny Chinese cars, scooters, and old women on black bicycles all jockeying for position. Ma was right; drivers would need insurance.

He started Ping An (which translates as "peace"), an insurance company that initially had little to insure and was dealing with a demographic that didn't even understand the concept of insurance. In 1993 Ping An moved past cars and into life insurance, an even bigger challenge. At first the agents didn't understand what they were selling, making it impossible to interest consumers. Ma brought in people from Taiwan to train his agents. After a year, Ma became the first Chinese insurer to bring foreign shareholders (Goldman Sachs, Morgan Stanley) on board. They provided a capital injection to facilitate expansion, and provided western corporate governance, which helped Ping An later on. At that point, the fledgling insurance industry in China was essentially a version of the Wild West.

By 2004, Ping An was one of the largest insurers in China. On an average day, they issued 34,417 policies, received 42,000 customer calls, and paid out several million dollars. They now have 450,000 sales agents and pioneered Internet and tele-sales.

Ping An was perfectly poised for China's entry to the World Trade Organization in 2001, when the insurance business suddenly took off. In 2004, they floated a successful IPO on the Hong Kong Stock Exchange. Their aim is to be a leading global financial services group.

One concept that is entrenched in the Chinese psyche is longevity. (One reason insurance was a hard sell, one observer noted, was that everyone thinks they're going to live to be a thousand.) China's history is told in terms of dynasties. Ma's company adopted the principle of longevity and is looking to the long term – not only expanding into banking but looking internationally as well.

Ma has blended the best of western management practices with Chinese values, and this hybrid has attracted both top executives and millions of customers. He has developed passion capital by recognizing a need before it existed, by establishing a company that had a clear mandate, by creating a corporate culture that is effective and binding, and by developing a strategy that continued past the vast expanse of his own country.

It took persistence to build a business that went against both the culture and the emphatic lack of physical need (no cars to insure). But Ma, one of China's first passion capitalists, saw where the country was going and was able to get there first.

Here are five suggestions for how to develop the persistence that helps create passion capital:

1. FIND THE NOBILITY IN TRYING

We live in a world that is hyper-competitive and overly focused on short-term success. In order to develop persistence it is vital to learn a simple lesson. "Trying is good. Trying again is better." Nothing of value is ever achieved without trial and error.

2. JUST IMAGINE

As children we celebrate our imagination. But too often as adults we lose that quality. Failing is often just a lack of imagination. The human imagination is capable of finding the solution to any problem – it just takes time. Our imagination needs to be trained, appreciated, and exercised just like our muscles. Persistence requires strength of imagination. Don't quit; keep imagining.

3. PATIENCE IS INDEED A VIRTUE

I am an avid fisherman. Every person who has baited a hook understands the importance of patience when it comes to catching tonight's dinner. In our world, everyone is rushing somewhere or trying to multi-task in the hopes of succeeding. How many times have fishermen quit just as the giant sea trout began to swim their way? Companies often fire their CEO in similar circumstances. Find, instill, and reward patience.

4. TAKE THE LONG VIEW

Malcolm Gladwell wrote convincingly about the ten thousand hours required as a minimum to master something. It takes a long time to do anything of value. Overnight success is almost always a myth and usually not sustainable when achieved. Think about sticking with your passion for years or decades. It will make the daily or weekly ups and downs seem like the minor blips they are. Passion helps sustain you with your long view.

5. FAITH

You never study or learn about "faith" in a business school. Yet persistence is grounded in faith – faith in yourself, your career, your company, your cause, or your country. Faith in your creed can sustain you. When you "keep the faith" in your passion, persistence becomes an enjoyable journey.

Weathering the Storms

Individual persistence is what usually drives start-ups; few ventures run smoothly right from the beginning. Often success comes not to the person with the best idea but to the one who is most persistent. You see this in every walk of life, from business to entertainment to romance (what is *she* doing with *him*?) to medicine. The world is filled with examples of individual persistence.

But persistence seems to be on the wane in the corporate world. Rather than stick with a philosophy or a CEO, there is a tendency to switch courses if there aren't immediate results. According to consulting firm Booz Allen Hamilton, between 1995 and 2006, CEO turnover increased by 59 per cent. In 2010, it jumped another 23.7 per cent. Leaders are staying in their jobs for shorter and shorter periods. The average lifespan of a

CEO for a Fortune 500 company is less than four years. Part of the reason for this trend is the demand for short-term results. A CEO is brought in to effect immediate change. If change is too slow, or isn't measured in ways the market appreciates, he is given a handsome severance, then someone else is brought in to (hopefully) turn the company around.

This strategy is counterproductive on several levels. First, it squanders resources on the golden parachutes given to departing executives. Second, time is lost while a new leader either adapts to the existing culture or implements a new one. Third, the short-term mentality kills long-term ambition.

The need for short-term results usually comes from pressure on a company's share price. In some cases, the analysts who cover specific stocks have become the modern equivalent of shamans. Mysterious and worshipped, they issue broad recommendations and deliver expectations on earnings and profit. Their advice can have a serious impact on a stock. It takes persistence to weather the storms that are sometimes stirred up by an analyst's comments. It can be difficult to resist these short-term pressures.

The problem with analysts' dictates is that they are only opinions. In some cases, they are influenced by self-interest. In 2003, the Securities and Exchange Commission brought a lawsuit against Morgan Stanley, alleging that between 1999 and 2001, it "engaged in acts and practices that created conflicts of interest for its research analysts with respect to investment banking activities and considerations." Essentially Morgan Stanley was using analysts' coverage as a marketing tool to gain investment banking business. The analysts, SEC lawyers argued, weren't able to look at a stock objectively. Their recommendations were untrustworthy, possibly misleading.

This possibility for conflict exists, either overtly or covertly, throughout the market. An extreme example was the case of short-seller Carson Block, whose company Muddy Waters warned in 2011 that Chinese forestry giant Sino-Forest was essentially a fraud. Muddy Waters was only a year old as a company, and had only one employee – Block. And Block had shorted Sino-Forest and stood to benefit if the stock went down. Even though he was an obscure analyst without a track record, and even though he didn't provide any hard evidence, after his announcement, Sino-Forest lost $3 billion in market cap in two days.

The fallout extended past Sino-Forest as other Chinese companies came under suspicion. Trading was suspended on Duoyuan Printing and China Electric Motor, among other companies. Warnings were issued for Chinese companies listed on U.S. exchanges, and some brokerages refused to allow clients to buy Chinese stocks on margin.

There were two issues here. The first was ostensibly whether Chinese accounting practices were up to the same standards as North American ones. The long-held suspicion was that they were not. But there is a long-held suspicion that North American standards aren't up to North American standards either. The endless list of Madoffs, Enrons, and Tycos has extended to Lehman Brothers and the Anglo Irish Bank. There is an underlying fear that many North American companies aren't playing by the rules. And after waves of deregulation, there aren't that many rules any more.

The dictum that the market runs on fear and greed has never been truer. That fear was magnified in the case of

Chinese stocks because of the opacity of those companies. It was difficult to get reliable information, so the fear factor increased. All of this makes for a climate that breeds fear and opportunism. Analysts suggest we need to buy Chinese stocks because it's the fastest-growing market in the world, with the largest upside. But buying them means living with fear.

The second, more illuminating issue was the impact one person can have on a company, or on an entire market. A few days after Block issued his accusation that Sino-Forest was a fraud, one of his allegations was disproved. He had argued that Sino-Forest overstated its revenues because it was physically unable to transport the number of logs it would have to ship to generate that kind of revenue. But 95 per cent of its stated revenues came from buying and selling standing timber, which means it isn't logging the trees, merely reselling the forest. But the facts didn't matter. Evidence eventually did come in against Sino-Forest, but by that time the stock had lost 82 per cent of its value. People didn't sell on the evidence, they sold on rumour and fear. That billions of dollars would vanish or shift on the word of someone who is an unknown and who has a stated conflict of interest speaks to the essential nature of the market: it is a fearful, skittish thing.

"The market is always right" is a dictum that's been around since Adam Smith. Perhaps in the final analysis, it's true. But there is no final analysis; the market is a continuum. At any specific point, the market can be distorted, hysterical, manipulated, or just plain wrong. And while the market isn't always right, it can be the final word.

In some ways, the market is an argument between traders and builders. The builder needs to view the long term, to withstand short-term pressures in order to achieve something worthwhile. The trader needs to realize the best return in the shortest time. Traders are always looking for the exit. For builders there is no exit.

As Geoff Beattie, the president of the Woodbridge Company, noted, traders aren't necessarily committed to the strategy of the companies they're invested in. What they want is to leverage the company's assets for quick gains. Sometimes they engage in shareholder activism to compel companies to take action to get short-term gains. Then they sell and move on to the next target.

For builders who need capital to create growth and stability and plan for the future, the pressure to accede to shareholders' immediate demands can be great. When companies feel pressure to calm rattled investors, they sometimes abandon their long-term plans. Staying the course takes courage and persistence, but staying the course is absolutely necessary in order to get out of the destructive cycle of short-term thinking and actions. Passion capital needs long-term planning and growth to prosper.

Peter Ma is a long-term thinker who is planning far into the future, while Carson Black is after a short-term gain that is disruptive, predatory, and, over the long term, unsustainable.

Politics as Usual

Politics faces some of the same short-term pressures as the corporate world. The four-year terms have shrunk perilously; for leaders, the first year in office is spent complaining about the mess they've inherited and the final year is spent in campaign mode. The two years in between are often spent whipsawing between poll numbers.

It isn't a recipe for productivity. Who wants to take a chance on an ambitious long-term project that could come to term under another party's banner? As a result there is a perpetual short-term mentality that is crippling initiative and ambition. It used to be that campaigns were short on substance – reduced to slogans, promises, and polls. But now governments are as well.

In Europe, Greece was bailed out by the European Union and the International Monetary Fund after its debt level became unsustainable. But Greece's problems are endemic, dating back to the Ottoman Empire. The two most glaring issues are rampant tax evasion (attributed to centuries of living under foreign rule, in which tax evasion was seen as a civic duty) and a bloated and inefficient government bureaucracy.

It would be fair to say that both the private and public sector went through a phase where there was no grasp of economic reality. Now both sectors are facing significant challenges, not just in Greece but everywhere. In some ways, they are opposites. The public sector is short on innovation but has responsibilities to society. The private sector possesses innovative ideas, but few of them are directed toward the larger benefit of society.

Passion capital is a bridge between these two poles. It takes the best from each sector – the sense of social responsibility from the government side combined with private sector efficiencies. There are tentative movements from western governments to lure private capital and initiative to deal with social issues.

In 2000, British prime minister Tony Blair established the Social Investment Task Force, which looked at proposals from the private sector that would address social issues. Sir Ronald Cohen, a British venture capitalist, was appointed head of the task force. Cohen had made his money by investing in start-ups like PPL Therapeutics (which cloned Dolly the sheep) and Virgin Radio. But when Blair's Labour government didn't implement any of the strategies, Cohen sought other means, venturing into what he calls "social capital." He started funding businesses in the poorest parts of Britain, and is also working on attracting investment to the West Bank and Gaza in the Middle East. "A whole sea change is beginning to start where the values that existed in business are being transported to social activity," he has said.

What Cohen and others are doing is the essence of passion capital. It is a bridge between private sector business skills and the passion that traditionally exists in not-for-profit initiatives. The philanthropic world has long had passion, whether it was to cure cancer, eradicate heart disease, fund an art gallery, or build schools in Africa.

The last golden age of philanthropy was during John D. Rockefeller's time, when he, Andrew Carnegie, Cornelius Vanderbilt Whitney, and other wealthy Americans gave extraordinary sums to build those aspects of the country that weren't being built – whether libraries (Carnegie built 2509 libraries, including 125 in Canada), museums (the Whitney Museum of American Art, the first museum to showcase

American art exclusively), or universities (Rockefeller gave $34 million to build the University of Chicago).

There is hope that the current crop of oligarchs will replicate that record. Roughly 1 per cent of the U.S. population controls 42 per cent of the country's wealth, the largest disparity in history and a potentially disastrous equation. The government is hoping to tap into some of that money.

When Barack Obama took office he created the Office of Social Innovation and Civic Participation. As part of an initiative to direct private sector innovation toward social issues, he also started the Social Innovation Fund, which began with a modest $50 million and attracted another $74 million from philanthropic foundations. The broad mandate is to give money to innovative not-for-profit organizations for work in healthcare, job creation, and youth education.

Britain's Prime Minister David Cameron unveiled a vision for a "Big Society" that is similar to Obama's idea. What he wants is to "open up public services to new providers like charities, social enterprises, and private companies so we get more innovation, diversity, and responsiveness to public need."

Neither the private nor the public sector has had a glorious run. But they can both benefit from these kinds of associations that span the two and use the best of each side.

The rampant deregulation by American and other western governments has helped fuel a short-term mentality. The last time an American government was able to move forward with significant long-term infrastructure and policy was probably during Franklin Roosevelt's four terms. But he had the luxury of that stretch in office. In Britain, that sense of long-term planning may go back to Margaret Thatcher, who made unpopular short-term decisions for future gain. It isn't a particular ideology that is right (you don't get much farther apart than FDR and the Iron Lady), but the philosophy of thinking over the long term.

When leaders are asked about their own role models, the politician who is often cited as an influence is Nelson Mandela. He might be the gold standard for political persistence: it took him half a century to win his battle against apartheid. He started his fight in 1948, after the election of the National Party, which supported the policy of segregation. He initially pursued his goal through peaceful means, then as a last resort became leader of the African National Congress's armed wing. They directed their violence at places rather than people, planning to blow up electrical, water, and gas utilities. Mandela was accused of treason and spent the next twenty-seven years in jail.

In jail he worked in a lime quarry, but he also took a correspondence course with the University of London and he received a law degree. In 1985, South African president P. W. Botha offered Mandela his freedom if he would publicly renounce violence as a political tool. Mandela turned him down and returned to prison, saying, "What freedom am I being offered while the organization of the people remains banned?"

Mandela was finally granted clemency by President F. W. de Klerk, who succeeded Botha, and was released in 1990. De Klerk also reversed the ban on anti-apartheid organizations, and in 1994 South Africa saw its first multiracial elections. The fight that Mandela had started forty-six years earlier had finally been won.

No one wants to wait half a century any more. But today's combination of short-term government planning and partisan paralysis has left many countries crippled with debt and incapable of action. In politics, persistence is a virtue that exists only through the lengthy election campaigns.

Writing with Passion

Novelist John Updike wrote that every book is an act of faith. At some point the author wonders if it is worth finishing, if it will find a publisher, if it will interest readers. There are so many reasons not to finish. It takes persistence to continue. It took Joseph Heller twelve years to write *Catch-22*. It takes another kind of persistence to get a book published. Heller's book was originally titled *Catch-18*; he increased the number with each rejection letter from uninterested publishers.

Margaret Mitchell's *Gone With the Wind* was turned down by thirty-eight publishers, then went on to become one of the bestselling books of all time. Stephen King's first book, *Carrie*, went out to thirty now regret-filled publishers before it found a home.

T. E. Lawrence – Lawrence of Arabia – lost the manuscript for his book *The Seven Pillars of Wisdom* when he was changing trains in Reading Station. It was never recovered. To write a book is a difficult thing. To write a book that you've already written is even more difficult. That thrill of discovery that existed the first time is gone. But Lawrence sat down and rewrote the entire book from memory. It went on to become a bestseller and was the basis for the 1962 film *Lawrence of Arabia*.

J. K. Rowling sent her first *Harry Potter* to nine publishers, all of whom turned it down. Nine professionals in the publishing industry agreed that it wasn't worth publishing. Why would a single mother on welfare with no writing experience believe that she was right and they were wrong? Perhaps she didn't. Maybe her faith was shaken by those rejections.

Forbes estimates Rowling's wealth to be more than $1 billion, and she is the first author in history to become a billionaire from writing. The franchise – books, films, and merchandise – is worth more than $10 billion. What if she hadn't sent the book out to that tenth (prescient) publisher? Hundreds of people found lucrative employment in the films, manufacturing the merchandise, distributing the books. The secondary and tertiary effects of a phenomenon like this echo through the economy. A hit like *Harry Potter* allows the publisher to take a chance elsewhere. Its commercial success can finance innovation. Literary books that may not have been otherwise published owe their life to Rowling's boy wizard.

Rowling wrote the first *Harry Potter* in a café with her baby in a stroller beside her. Not ideal conditions for writing. Her persistence, not just in the act of creation but in pushing her creation out into the world, was the crucial difference.

Finding a Cure

The French scientist and researcher Louis Pasteur said, "My strength lies solely in my tenacity." Pasteur is most remembered for inventing a method to make milk safe, using the process that now bears his name – pasteurization.

Pasteur wasn't the person who discovered germ theory, but he was the one who pursued the idea through endless experiments and was able to then sell the idea to a skeptical Europe. Selling the idea was critical because medical innovation isn't any use unless it's adopted. Pasteur had passion with a strategy, and this allowed a scientific breakthrough to become a practical innovation. He showed the world that the growth of bacteria was what spoiled milk.

Pasteur's career as a medical innovator was wide ranging, but all his work was marked by his doggedness. He pursued a cure for typhoid because he had lost three of his five children to the disease. He was infused with a passion to help prevent other children from dying.

Medical research, perhaps more than any other endeavour, has relied on persistence. The journey toward a cure for cancer has been a long one – the first mastectomy was performed in 1882. Six years later Marie Curie discovered radium, and a few years later it was used to treat cancer patients. If you examine the timeline for cancer breakthroughs, two things become clear. One is that the people responsible for groundbreaking research come from various countries and scientific backgrounds; it is a global and multidisciplinary effort. The second thing is that significant progress is being made at increasingly shorter intervals. From the turn of the twentieth century to the early 1940s there weren't many developments. But then they start coming more quickly. In 1943, the first electron linear accelerator designed for radiation therapy was developed, and it is now the most widely used medical device in world. After that there is a new development almost every year, from sequencing DNA (1975) to the discovery of oncogenes (1976) to anti-nausea drugs for chemotherapy (1980).

In cancer research, there has always been individual persistence, but now there is an institutional persistence as well. The challenge of raising money to support that research requires the same kind of determination. Perhaps the most inspirational and influential example of fundraising comes from Terry Fox.

On April 12, 1980, when Terry began his cross-country run to raise money and awareness for cancer, few people took notice. He was a twenty-two-year-old who had lost one leg to the disease, an athlete who was attempting an impossible feat. His Marathon of Hope began in St. John's, Newfoundland, and Terry essentially ran a marathon every day. In the Maritimes, he was a curiosity and was almost run off the road on occasion. But by the time he got to Ontario, people were taking notice.

When he was originally diagnosed with osteosarcoma, Terry was told he had a 50 per cent chance of survival. But only two years earlier the chances of survival were 15 per cent. This fact made an impression on him. He realized how much had happened in such a short time, and he found out that cancer research was underfunded. Because he felt he owed his life to medical advances, he became determined to raise money to fund more research.

Fox's run was the epitome of persistence. It was painful due to his artificial leg, and it would have been a gruelling run even for a two-legged marathoner. His initial goal was to raise $1 million. He later raised that goal to $24 million, with the idea that each of Canada's 24 million people could contribute a dollar.

When he got to Toronto, ten thousand people gathered to cheer him on. He raised $100,000 that day. Hockey legend Bobby Orr gave him another $25,000. On September 1, it was discovered that his cancer had progressed. He ran 3339 miles before the cancer spread to his lungs, forcing him to quit near Thunder Bay. He had raised $1.7 million. But a week later a telethon was held to support Fox and the Canadian Cancer Society, and it raised a further $10.5 million. By the following April, a year after he'd begun his marathon, the total was more than $23 million.

By June the cancer had spread further; Terry Fox fell into a coma and died on June 28, 1981.

The first annual Terry Fox Run was held that year. It has grown over the decades and is now held in sixty countries. The event is the world's largest one-day fundraiser for cancer research. To date the Terry Fox Run has raised more than $500 million.

Persistence is born of belief: you believe the book you're working on is worth writing, that the medical research you're conducting will help mankind, that your invention will revolutionize an industry, that your marathon will raise money. As T. Boone Pickens said, offering his Oklahoma oilman spin, "If you're on the right side of the issue, just keep driving until you hear glass breaking. Don't quit."

KEY LESSONS

1. Persistence is the determination and will to keep working toward something you believe in. Persistence is the heart of passion capital.

2. Persistence is the vehicle that transports us from loss, blockage, and defeat to a fresh starting point.

3. Persistence is both an attitude (patience) and a learned skill (imagination).

4. Persistence is born in belief and self-sacrifice, often in the service of a greater good.

9

MANAGEMENT AND LEADERSHIP:

PUTTING PASSION TO WORK

Management is doing things right;
leadership is doing the right things.
PETER DRUCKER

In the world of sport, you often hear the phrase "a passion for winning." Sometimes it's applied to a player, or a team, or to a new coach who has come in to turn things around. Sometimes this passion translates into victory. Most of the time, however, it doesn't.

The essence of management is to create impact and value, and few businesses show this essence as clearly as sports. Every manager inherits a team. But he also gets to choose new players, through the draft, by trading, or by bringing up young talent from the minor leagues. He then implements a strategy, either basing a new one on his current resources or reusing one he has used successfully elsewhere. Sometimes he inherits a culture; other times he's been brought in to create or impose one. The results of all these efforts can be clearly measured in terms of wins and losses.

The first thing a new manager does when he arrives is assess the team's strengths and weaknesses. Are they weak on defence? Do they need an offensive threat? Maybe it's a young team and they need veteran leadership. And there is the question of money. Who can you afford to bring in? How do you build a team?

In looking at two National Hockey League teams – the Montreal Canadiens and the Toronto Maple Leafs – over the last fifty years, we see two very different organizations. They differ in strategy, in management style, in leadership, and most profoundly, in results. The Canadiens possess passion capital and are ostensibly the more successful organization, but the Leafs are a fascinating contrast.

The early years of the two clubs were similar. During what has been called the golden era of the six-team league (1942–67), they both enjoyed periods of dominance, and they regularly vied for the Stanley Cup. Theirs was an intense and entertaining rivalry. But in 1967, the two teams began to diverge. The Canadiens refined a management style that had worked so well for them, while the Leafs chose a new path.

Management and leadership aren't always clearly defined in sport. Management is usually considered to be the general manager, while leadership is supplied by the head coach. In the case of the Maple Leafs, however, Harold Ballard, who became part owner in 1957 and sole owner in 1972, essentially filled both roles for many years. He owned both the team and its home arena, Maple Leaf Gardens.

For most of the years when Ballard shared ownership, he wasn't involved in managing the team. His chief responsibility was running the building, and he displayed a canny if ruthless business sense. When the Beatles played there in 1965, Ballard sold tickets for two shows, even though the Beatles had agreed to only one. Fearing a mob scene, they ended up playing the second show.

Ballard didn't have much to do with the actual team until 1967, the last year the Leafs won a Stanley Cup. Immediately after that championship game, Ballard sold the team's two minor-league affiliates, the Victoria Cougars and the Rochester Americans, leaving the Leafs without a pool of young talent to draw on. And this at a time when the Leafs were the oldest team in the league: the Stanley Cup champions had six players over the age of thirty-six, two of them over forty. The Leafs also had one of the smallest scouting budgets in the National Hockey League. Ballard didn't believe in spending money on research and development. His reasoning was short-sighted: we're the champions, we don't need to seek out new talent.

The following year, the Royal Canadian Mounted Police began an investigation into the team's finances, and in 1972 Ballard was convicted of forty-seven counts of fraud for taking money from Maple Leaf Gardens. He spent a year in jail. He then assumed sole ownership of the Maple Leafs after one of his two partners sold his shares and the other one died. Now the team was all his.

For the next eighteen years Ballard was the one enduring icon of the Maple Leafs. He fired ten coaches in those years, several general managers, and key players he took a dislike to. During his reign, only two teams had a worse record than the Leafs. For five of those years they had not only the worst winning percentage in hockey but one of the worst winning percentages in sport, finishing 121st out of 122 professional teams in basketball, baseball, football, and hockey.

Ballard used to say that he was laughing all the way to the bank. And perhaps he was. But it's hard to believe that money was the central issue. He didn't have ostentatious tastes. His only hobby, oddly, given that he lived in the mausoleum of Maple Leaf Gardens, was gardening, which he did at his cottage. And although he made money, he didn't make nearly as much as he could have with better management. In 1976, ticket sales reached a peak of $2 million, but a decade later, after the team's worst stretch, sales had dropped to $1.4 million. There were limits even to Leafs fans' now legendary tolerance for loss.

The fall of the Leafs was all the more impressive because until Ballard's ownership they had one of the most distinguished histories of any sports franchise. They were among the elite that includes the Montreal Canadiens, New York Yankees, and Pittsburgh Steelers. At the outset Ballard was more interested in the team's economic possibilities than its hockey operation. He didn't really see the relationship between the two. Ballard embodied the idea that short-term planning can lead to disastrous long-term consequences.

Ballard believed that the Toronto market was so large and hungry that he could fill Maple Leaf Gardens for every game regardless of the on-ice product – and the market, for the most part, proved him right. But if Ballard was cynical, he was also extremely competitive. He wanted to win. Yet no owner has a record of losing that rivals Ballard's. How did it happen?

The structural problems were certainly part of it. Without a farm team the Leafs sacrificed new talent. But the larger problem was that Ballard assumed the role of both leader and manager. He believed that he understood the game better than any of his beleaguered coaches. He liked players who hit, who fought, and he tended to hire coaches who were journeymen. He was suspicious of finesse, innovation, and leadership. The only coach of notable merit that he hired was Roger Nielson, a pioneering hockey mind and the first coach to use videotape to analyze performance. Under Nielson, a genuine team took shape: Darryl Sittler, Lanny McDonald, Ian Turnbull, Börje Salming, and Mike Palmateer in goal. They were a force and made it to the semifinals, but Ballard quickly disassembled them, firing Nielson and trading Sittler and McDonald, his two stars. To replace Nielson, he hired John Brophy, a former pugilist from the minor leagues.

One Gardens employee observed that Ballard got rid of anyone who knew hockey. "He wanted to run it his way. When Nielson came in with his scientific methods, Ballard said, 'We don't need that.' He called him the Video Man. He didn't like anyone smart. If they went to college, Ballard didn't like them."

In trying to analyze the perverse leadership of Harold Ballard, a few sportswriters thought that the central problem was the man's ego. He competed with players and coaches for publicity and so he traded popular players and charismatic coaches because they overshadowed him. There is some truth to that.

But a larger problem was that Ballard cared less about victory, which he couldn't dictate, than exercising power, which he could. Ultimately, his passion wasn't for winning but for power. We see this in sport as well as in the corporate world.

Sometimes to win the war, you need to lose some of the internal battles. Ballard lost on the ice but won every battle in the organization. In his clashes with employees, he was undefeated. To achieve victory on the ice, Ballard would have had to have lost some of the battles off the ice, something he was too stubborn to allow.

It wasn't just Ballard's hockey knowledge that was lacking. His business abilities also diminished notably. He failed to grasp how important the marketing of team products was becoming, growing from a sideline to a multi-million-dollar business. The venue, which he owned, was badly in need of upgrades, but Ballard refused to spend the money, even though he also lived there. He was without any kind of strategy for the long term, from either a team perspective or a purely business perspective.

Ballard didn't understand the dynamics of team sports. He didn't see the Leafs as an ecosystem where changes would reverberate throughout the organization, where development and continuity were critical. He saw players and coaches as interchangeable parts that could be moved at random.

He also turned his back on the Leafs' glorious past. Ballard didn't allow the retired sweaters of the team's stars to be displayed in the Gardens and wouldn't even allow the eleven Stanley Cup banners that preceded his ownership to hang in the arena. He destroyed the culture that had existed and replaced it with one of mediocrity.

The week after he died, in 1990, there were immediate changes to the dysfunctional culture at Maple Leaf Gardens. The Stanley Cup banners went up. The Gardens employees, who were the lowest paid in the league, got a long overdue

52 per cent raise. An alumni lounge was built for retired players (many of whom had been banished from the Gardens). Sportswriters cheered the beginning of a new era; the Leafs would finally return to their winning ways.

Yet they didn't. The organization never recovered. More than twenty years later, Ballard's stamp remains on the team. In the richest hockey market in the world, the Leafs haven't won a championship in forty-four years, and their winning record remains one of the worst in hockey.

Let's look at the Montreal Canadiens during the same period. In those fifty years they won twelve Stanley Cups and have one of the best records in hockey. In Montreal the ownership was hands-off, and took no part in the operation of the team. The hierarchy was clear. They tended to hire from within the organization. For twenty-four of the last twenty-seven years, the general manager has been a former Habs player. Dozens of former Canadiens have worked with the organization (Serge Savard, Jean Béliveau, Réjean Houle, Bob Gainey), and many others have gone to other organizations where they have imported their ethic and excelled. Jacques Lemaire and Larry Robinson brought the Stanley Cup to New Jersey as coaches. Scotty Bowman, who won five Stanley Cups with Montreal as coach, went on to win one as the coach of Pittsburgh, and then three more with the Detroit Red Wings.

The Canadiens started with a motto that is written in the dressing room: "To you from failing hands we throw the torch. Be yours to hold it high." Taken from John McCrae's poem "In Flanders Fields," it emphasizes the team's rich tradition;

since its inception, the Canadiens have won more Stanley Cups (twenty-four) than any other hockey team, and they are one of the most successful franchises in sport. Only the mighty New York Yankees have won more championships (twenty-seven).

Because the Canadiens routinely finished at or near the top of the standings, they rarely got the first-draft picks, which tend to be in inverse order of the standings (that is, the worst team gets first pick) in order to provide some parity in the league. This would seem, on the surface, to be a disadvantage. The next superstar will always be going somewhere else. Yet it proved to be an advantage because the team had to rely on continuity, on developing talent, and became adept at trades.

The culture created in the Canadiens organization was based on nurturing talent, respecting tradition, and building to win. In what was a glaringly lopsided trade in the 1980s, Montreal traded enforcer John Kordic to the Toronto Maple Leafs for Russ Courtnall, a prolific scorer and one of the fastest skaters in the league. Each team was pursuing a specific strategy. Montreal wanted the speed and finesse that were their hallmark. For the Leafs, it was the opposite. They were still living by former Leaf owner Conn Smythe's famous dictum, "If you can't beat 'em in the alley, you won't beat 'em on the ice." There may have been a time when this was true, but the Leafs were pursuing an outdated strategy.

Montreal used passion capital to propel their team to success. They started with a strong creed, created a culture that has lasted a century, and implemented successful strategies. As both an organization and a team, they were innovative, were closely knit, looked to the long term, and developed from within.

The Leafs, on the other hand, were almost a nineteenth-century version of capitalism, with a stingy eccentric owner who could see only profit and short-term gain. There was no clear management hierarchy, and any leadership was com-promised by Ballard's heavy-handed interference. Ballard hired undistinguished or even incompetent people, and he then benefited in comparison.

And this is where the story ends. Except for one critical detail. Which team is worth more? The Toronto Maple Leafs, it turns out, are the most valuable team in hockey, estimated by *Forbes* to be worth $505 million, with revenues of $187 mil-lion. Montreal was in third place, worth $408 million, with revenues of $163 million.

Which team is more successful?

The goals of the two teams aren't the same, and so suc-cess can't be measured by the same yardstick. The Montreal Canadiens have been owned for much of the modern era by the Molson family, which has been an integral part of that city's corporate culture since 1782. The team embodies the city – it even has a political dimension. When Rocket Richard was suspended in 1955, the ensuing riot in Montreal had as much to do with francophone rights as it did with hockey. The Canadiens are embedded in the community. Their style of play, which for much of its history has been characterized by elegant passing and fast skating, reflects the stylish city. It is profitable, and it is a perennial competitor. Part of the Canadiens' goal is to represent the community, which it has done as admirably as any sports team in history.

By contrast, the Maple Leafs were majority owned by Maple Leaf Sports and Entertainment, which was 80 per cent owned by the Ontario Teachers' Pension Plan. While both groups want to make money, an investment fund doesn't have the same goals as a local family. The Leafs didn't make the playoffs in the 2010/2011 season, and weren't particularly entertaining. But they were profitable. From a leadership perspective, Maple Leaf Sports and Entertainment accomplished the critical goal.

People who are in the same business don't necessarily have the same goals. It is the leader's job to define those goals.

The Maple Leafs don't need passion capital. They can roll along in the existing model because of the size of the market and the fact that it's a closed market; the league won't allow a competing team in Toronto. If it did, the Leafs would probably need to adapt to a free market economy, and there would likely be changes to both the organization and the team.

The Canadiens, on the other hand, are an example of passion capital and continue to operate that way. It remains one of the most profitable hockey organizations, but the team transcends hockey, and has a beneficial impact on the community in political, social, and philanthropic ways.

It Starts with People

Usually the first job for any manager in sport is hiring the right players. Choosing the right personnel always looks easy in hindsight, but even Wayne Gretzky wasn't a slam dunk. Although he'd been a boy wonder in junior hockey, some scouts said he wouldn't have much impact in the NHL; he was too frail, and he'd get crushed (he routinely finished last among his Oiler teammates in strength tests).

Tom Brady, of the New England Patriots, is one of the few quarterbacks to have played in four Super Bowls, winning three of them, and he was chosen as MVP in two of them. He is considered one of the greatest passers of all time. Yet he was the 199th player chosen in the draft. Virtually no one saw his potential when he entered the league.

Kurt Warner, another brilliant quarterback and Super Bowl MVP, wasn't even drafted. The hundreds of college players selected didn't include him. He laboured in the Arena Football League, essentially a novelty act, and worked at a supermarket bagging groceries. When he finally got a shot at the NFL, he shone, and today holds several passing records.

Yet quarterbacks that were chosen in the first round or were number-one picks have been busts (Art Schlichter, Ryan Leaf, Tim Couch). These choices can reverberate within an organization for years. Not only are large sums of money wasted (Ryan Leaf had a four-year, $31.25-million deal, with an $11.25 million signing bonus), but there is a salary cap in the NFL. It's a zero-sum game. Even if you had the money, you couldn't spend it on another prospect. And trading them is difficult, because their contract goes with them and no one wants to pick up that tab. You're stuck with your decision.

Some of the players who have disappointed when they got to the big leagues simply didn't have the right stuff. They may have been stars in high school and college, but management failed to recognize weaknesses or tendencies that could be a problem when faced with professionals. In the case of quarterback Doug Flutie, the converse was true. A star at Boston College, where he won the Heisman Trophy, he was thought to be too small for the NFL. He finally went to the Canadian Football League, where he was a star, and then returned to the NFL, where he demonstrated that his athleticism, intelligence, and running ability easily compensated for his lack of size.

But above all, Flutie had a genuine passion to win. Passion is an intangible. General managers have all kinds of technical aids in assessing talent. Every sport quantifies hard data: What is his speed in the 40-yard dash? How fast is his fastball? What percentage of his outside shots did he hit in college? The NFL is the richest sport in the United States and has the deepest and most sophisticated scouting systems. Few players with talent at the high school level go undetected. By the time a college player reaches the draft, there is literally a book on him. There are charts that look like the technical analysis of a stock, showing intersecting lines and moving averages and charting expected gains. How is it that managers can still get it so wrong?

Ultimately, assembling a team is more art than science. There is no quantitative way to measure passion, and if there was, it doesn't always translate into winning. You still need strategy and persistence and a winning culture. But often passion is a determining factor. It was for Doug Flutie and Tom Brady and Kurt Warner and for Gretzky and Michael Jordan. All of them possessed great skills, but what set them apart was a passion to win that was palpable in their play, especially in important games. That passion was infectious; it lifted the whole team.

Sometimes the reason everyone is going after a player is simply because everyone else is going after him. Can everyone else be wrong? They can, it turns out. You have to do your own homework when hiring personnel. In business, it comes down to asking the right questions. The CV is a great place to start, but not a great place to hire from. You need to talk to a person to get a sense of how much passion he or she has, and what that passion is for.

Some of the players who fell apart when they got to the major leagues had the right stuff, but they didn't fit into the team system or they clashed with management. On other teams, they might have shone. And many have. They were lacklustre on one team but suddenly overachieved when they were traded.

Again, management is implicated. They were unable to realize the potential of a player they went after. Or they weren't able to see that despite his obvious talents, he wasn't a good fit.

Management is an evolving art. Good managers are aware of new developments, of shifts in moods, of changes in culture or strategy. You see sports teams that were assembled for another time, a hockey team that put together a squad of tough guys who would have matched up well against the 1976 Philadelphia Flyers, but who look slow and clumsy against fast-skating teams filled with talented Europeans. Where is the zeitgeist going? You need to hire for what is coming next, not what happened last.

As you move farther up the chain in any organization, you have more senior people reporting to you. This presents challenges that didn't exist when you were managing labour. Tony Dungy, the brilliant former coach of the Indianapolis

Colts football team and now a TV analyst, was asked what the difference was between coaching college players and coaching pros. In college, he said, you're coaching twenty-two-year-old guys. In the pros, you're coaching twenty-three-year-old millionaires.

It's a critical difference. The balance of power has shifted somewhat, and management has to recognize that and find strategies to deal with it. It's hard to tell the marquee quarterback with the $11-million signing bonus to do ten laps.

Measuring Progress

In any business, as in sport, you need to be able to measure performance. This sometimes isn't as easy as it sounds. In sport, success is usually measured in championships. But in a thirty-team league, it isn't always true that there are twenty-nine unsuccessful teams at the end of the season. A team that moved up twelve places in the standings during the first year of a rebuilding phase can be said to have had a good season. They are working toward the future and made impressive gains. A championship team that traded talented young prospects to get a team of expensive veterans may be at the end of an era. They may have won the championship, but the next year their team will be too old to compete, and they've traded away the future. In terms of immediate reward, they are a success. But in the long term, it could be a generation before they fully recover.

We see the same thing with meeting quarterly targets as opposed to maintaining a sustainable long-term goal. Missing a quota doesn't necessarily mean failure. Good managers have to recognize the context, not just the numbers.

One reason for the continuing success of the Pittsburgh Steelers football team is that, like the Montreal Canadiens, they created a culture that has remained intact for decades. Formed in 1933, and still owned by the same family, the team developed a blue-collar culture that reflected the steelmaking city they represented. They weren't flashy, were big on defence, and had an enviable work ethic. Since 1972, the Steelers have made the playoffs a record twenty-five times. They have won twenty division titles and have six Super Bowl wins, the most in the NFL. They have rarely been the most talented team in the league, but they have always maximized their resources. They know who they are and what kind of player they are looking for. This self-knowledge has guided them toward long-term success.

Essentially, managing is implementing the seven principles of passion capital, but it all begins with belief. And belief arises from self-knowledge. One of the hallmarks of unsuccessful teams in any sport is the ever-changing approach to strategy and personnel. They concentrate on defence, then switch to being offensive-minded if that doesn't work. They draft individual stars rather than pick the person who is best suited to help the organization. The team is constantly rebuilding around a new talent and never really finds out who or what it is. Every season, a new series of clichés fails to motivate it.

Leading Questions

Leaders decide where you are heading; managers dictate how you'll get there. Leadership's first question is: Where do we want to go? With sport, the answer is usually: We want to win the championship. But this isn't always the case. Context is everything.

Much has been written about leadership styles. There are certainly lots to choose from. But you don't get to choose, or at least you shouldn't. The issue isn't whether you're a Dr. Phil let's-have-a-group-hug kind of leader or a thundering, threatening Gen. George S. Patton. The issue is authenticity.

Going against your own grain, against your personality, is like going against history; eventually you will lose. Leadership has to be genuine. Ken Thomson was an understated leader. He was reserved, dignified, and loyal, and people responded. T. Boone Pickens was in-your-face and rarely out of the public eye, but his leadership galvanized his company. Golda Meir was emotional, but she governed during an emotional time and Israelis responded to her emotion. Canada's first prime minister, John A. Macdonald, was drunk for weeks on end, though articulate and passionate about creating a country. When he ran against the sober George Brown, he said the country would "rather have John A. drunk than George Brown sober." He was right. Brown was a solid manager, but Macdonald had passion, and while voters understood the country would need both, at the delicate point of its creation, passion was the more critical ingredient.

Whether creating a country or a hockey team, passion is the most important ingredient. To marshal that passion, to get it working with common purpose toward a common goal, is the job of management and leadership. Muhammad Ali said, "Champions aren't made in the gym. Champions are made from something they have deep inside them – a desire, a dream, a vision."

Leaders need to identify that desire and articulate it, and give their team the tools necessary to achieve success. That's the essence of passion capital. We see it with Isadore Sharp and his philosophy, we see it with Dominic Barton and McKinsey. It's evident in the legacy that Ken Thomson left behind and in the creed of Johnson & Johnson. It exists in the corporate structures of Apple and Pixar, and in Ping An insurance. It is the final step to directing and maximizing passion capital.

KEY LESSONS

1. Passion capitalists understand that you lead people and manage things.

2. Leadership uses passion to create energy, make positive change, and win. Management uses the seven building blocks in the process of creating passion capital.

3. Leaders keep their eyes on tomorrow, and managers keep their eyes on today.

4. Great leaders are not necessarily great managers, and vice versa.

EPILOGUE

It is not length of life, but depth of life.
RALPH WALDO EMERSON

Growing up in Windsor, Ontario, right next to Detroit, I had a passion for music. You could feel the pulse coming across the Detroit River. Motown was there. There was a gospel scene, a jazz scene. As a kid I remembered Mitch Ryder and the Detroit Wheels. Then came Bob Seger, Iggy Pop, Madonna, Alice Cooper. Everyone who was my age in Windsor claims that Alice Cooper played at their high school. (He didn't play at mine but did play at Herman Collegiate.)

Music retailing was a natural fit for me. I brought the passion I'd felt for the music to the stores. I was able to create an environment at HMV where that passion was communicated. It drew others who were passionate about music, and it helped infuse a passion into casual customers. For those who worked there, it didn't feel like a retail job; it felt like something between a party and a movement. That's part of what made HMV the most successful music retailer in Canada. We held wonderful events that brought people in touch with the energy and personalities of the performers. From Alice Cooper to Tony Bennett, from Mariah Carey to the Ramones. Jazz, punk, classical, rap, rock, world, metal – all genres, all tastes, all types of music. There is a lot of nostalgia for that store and for that time. Shopping there was certainly a more social activity than downloading songs onto your iPod. But general systems theory prevailed. The environment changed, entropy and homeostasis lurked, and the music business changed. Now the HMV store on Yonge is one of the last retail music stores standing, smaller than it was in its heyday.

But I have changed as well. The music business was a young man's game. I'm no longer young. I still love music, but other things have become more important. My mother's death was a watershed moment. Going into the social profit sector was the right move for me. My passion had shifted, and raising money for cancer research became my goal, the thing I was most passionate about. I brought a lot of what I had learned about business to my job as CEO of the Princess Margaret Hospital Foundation. I have helped raise more than half a billion dollars. But I have learned even more in my time there, about business, about value, about people, and about life. One of the most powerful illustrations of the importance of what we do is seen on our annual Ride to Conquer Cancer.

At 6 a.m. on an unseasonably cool June day, hundreds of cyclists milled on the grounds of the Canadian National

Exhibition site in Toronto. By 7:30 there were thousands; a sea of yellow jerseys – the Princess Margaret Hospital Foundation jerseys for the Ride to Conquer Cancer. They were worn by cancer survivors and their families, by friends and supporters, by teenagers and octogenarians. They arrived with old clunkers and $10,000 racing bikes. But they were united in a single purpose: to conquer cancer in our lifetime. By 8 a.m., 4610 riders were assembled, and they had raised more than $17 million.

The annual ride began in 2008 as a two-day ride from Toronto to Niagara Falls. It was a huge success, raising $14.8 million, and the next year it became a national event. There are now rides between Vancouver and Seattle, between Montreal and Quebec City, and between Calgary and Banff. It is the largest two-day fundraiser for cancer in the country.

Organizing the event was a journey in and of itself. We conceived of the idea in 2005 and thought that to make the event a success we'd need to get Lance Armstrong's foundation LIVESTRONG involved. But we didn't realize the demands that are put on the foundation and on Lance. Unfortunately, we didn't have any luck negotiating with them and came away disappointed. Instead we went to the Chicago company that organizes Lance's cycling events in the United States – Event 360 – but after a year, we hadn't made much progress. We then went down to Boston to get advice from Billy Starr, who runs the Pan-Massachusetts Challenge, a cycling event that raises money for the Dana-Farber Cancer Institute in Boston. But that wasn't all that helpful either.

We finally decided to push ahead with our own resources. We linked up with CauseForce, a Los Angeles company that produces large-scale fundraising events for cancer. That relationship did work, and the first year was such a success that we quickly expanded to three other Canadian cities. To date, the Ride to Conquer Cancer has involved more than fifteen thousand riders and has raised almost $63 million in Toronto alone.

The Ride supports research programs such as the immuno-therapy program, the cancer stem cell program, and the tumour hypoxia program. It also supports research platforms and the one thousand staff that make the Princess Margaret one of the top five cancer research centres in the world. When riders register for the event, they are asked to select where they want their fundraising dollars to go.

The Ride is an emotional two days. The riders were cancer survivors themselves, or were riding for a friend or a family member. Each bike contained a story: of the disease, of our struggle to conquer it, of the challenges facing researchers and oncologists, of the fight to raise money to fund them.

One of the riders was a police officer named Steve Campbell, who had lost his wife, Linda, a year earlier. She had been battling breast and lung cancer for fifteen years and was admitted to hospital just days before the 2010 Ride. Steve started the event that year but heard partway through the ride that her condition had gotten worse. He left the ride to go to her side, and she died a few hours later. In 2011 he rode in memory of his wife.

Another rider was Dr. Robert Buckman, who worked at the Princess Margaret Hospital and was one of the most courageous and gifted clinicians and scientists that I've ever worked with. He was an avid supporter of our Ride to Conquer Cancer and used a unique (to fit his personality) three-wheeled bicycle. At the end of the ride, he said to me, "I need a cold beer, a hot bath, and a bigger hill next year, Alofs." He always sought a bigger hill.

In October 2011, Robert died unexpectedly in his sleep on a flight from London to Toronto. Like so many others whose lives he touched, I started to miss him immediately. His specialty was breast cancer and low-dose chemotherapy research, but he also had an enormous impact on the medical community through his teaching and writing.

His personal creed was that of a humanist who viewed both medicine and life with compassion, wisdom, and humour. His humour came naturally and was nurtured when he was a student at the University of Cambridge, where he participated in the Footlights Revue. Performing was something he kept up for his entire life.

In 1979, he was diagnosed with dermatomyositis, an autoimmune disease that was almost fatal. The experience influenced his work, and a string of books and television series followed, informed by his considerable medical wisdom, his own experience with the illness, and his humour. His energy was extraordinary and unflagging. He was president of the Humanist Association of Canada, and chair of the Advisory Board on Bioethics of the International Humanist and Ethical Union. He was an oncologist, professor, author, scientist, TV personality, and columnist. Few people have cut such a figure in so many different disciplines and done so with such wisdom and wit. We are left with his indelible image, in the form of books (among them, *Cancer is a Word, Not a Sentence*; *What You Really Need to Know About Cancer: A Guide for Patients and Their Families*; and *Can We*

Be Good Without God?: Behaviour, Belonging, and the Need to Believe). But for those who knew him personally, his legacy was one of extraordinary compassion.

Rob had a rare ability to communicate, which was reflected in his course on communicating with patients at the University of Toronto medical school, his television work, and his medical instructional videos with John Cleese of Monty Python fame. He had the courage to challenge the traditional ways that doctors communicated with their patients (for example, to volunteer as little information as possible), and he was able to find humour in the darkest of human moments.

There were entirely new stories on our Weekend to End Women's Cancers. The 60-kilometre walk has raised more than $112 million for research. More than four thousand people participated, 95 per cent of them women. One of the most remarkable was Kitty Cohen, who at ninety-eight had been participating for three years. Before she walks across the finish line she dances a jig. She has become a symbol for the weekend and an inspiration – if a woman approaching her hundredth birthday can do it, certainly others can.

⸙

When you're surrounded by cancer patients and their friends and family, you tend to focus on what is most valuable in life. It is hard to spend time with them and not ask yourself the questions they are asking themselves: What did I create? What do I value?

At the end of the day, playwright Arthur Miller said, all we can do is hope to end up with the right regrets. We don't want to leave knowing we didn't live life with passion. And we don't want to see that passion disappear either, to watch it die because we didn't know how to turn it into something tangible and memorable. The passion capital we create can live after us, can affect other lives for the better. I am grateful that I was able to realize this, and grateful that I've been given the opportunities to act on it.

Passion is a gift, a gift you can give to yourself, your company, your cause, or your country. Own your passion. Build your passion capital. Become a passion capitalist and you will be in possession of the world's most valuable asset.

ACKNOWLEDGEMENTS

I HAVE MANY PEOPLE TO THANK on this journey to becoming a passion capitalist and to completing this book.

First, I would like to thank my lovely and extraordinary wife, Sheila. She has always been an ongoing inspiration, both for the writing of this book and in our lives together. Sheila understood passion capital and helped me see the incredible power in this idea. Her three children, Noah, Jessica, and Daniel Geist, have also been inspirational, and generous with their encouragement and support. My son, James, and my daughter, Sarah, helped define and shape this book at every stage, from concept through to final edit, and this book would not have come together without them. James lives and works in Beijing and was extremely helpful in identifying stories of passion capitalists from Asia. Sarah, who is an associate with Boston Consulting Group in their Boston office, had nearly daily input into my work and has been instrumental in bringing clarity and focus to the book. James and Sarah are both passion capitalists, and I am grateful for their extraordinary contributions. My father, Omer Alofs, is an important contributor to my journey and to the book. My late mother, Pat Alofs, who passed away November 2, 2002, was the original passion capitalist in my life.

I'd like to acknowledge my late boss and mentor, Stuart McAllister, who was the chairman of HMV Group in the early days of my passion capital journey. Peter Luckhurst and Cathy Pitt, both executives with HMV, also played an important role in how this story evolved from its early stages, more than two decades ago.

I'd like to thank the early readers and believers in this work: Steve Bear, managing partner of McKinsey Canada; David Shaw, founder and CEO of Knightsbridge Human Capital; Diane Brisebois, head of the Retail Council of Canada; Kevin Lynch, vice-chairman of BMO and former Clerk of the Privy Council; Maureen Shaughnessy Kitts, formerly of McDonalds of Canada; Jack Fleischmann, head of BNN; Cheryl Reicin, senior partner of Torys; and Geoff Beattie, CEO of the Woodbridge Company and vice-chair of Thomson-Reuters. They all provided valuable input on the early draft of the book. Special acknowledgement and thank you to David Shaw and Leslie Carter of Knightsbridge Human Capital for leading the search for Canada's top passion capitalists.

I'd like to thank Don Gillmor for his support and research at all stages of the book. Don is a brilliant writer and storyteller. And thanks to the early connectors who provided important support, including my literary agent, Rick Broadhead, and members of Naked Creative Consultancy: Marc Giacomelli, Peter Shier, and Jim Whitney. Alistair Bruyns and Simon Plashkes of TenThousand have helped get the word out on passion capital in many creative ways.

It's important to recognize the Princess Margaret Hospital Foundation leadership, including Lionel Robins, Neville Kirchmann, Keith Ambachtsheer, John Bowey, and John MacNaughton. The passion capitalists of the medical community that I work so closely with have been an ongoing inspiration. Dr. Bob Bell is the CEO of University Health Network and quite possibly the finest CEO I have ever known. Dr. Mary Gospodarowicz is a gifted leader and heads the UICC in Geneva, the world's largest cancer control organization, as well as doing her work at Princess Margaret. Dr. Ben Neel is the brilliant research mind behind the global top-five standing for the Princess Margaret in cancer research. Ben left Harvard Medical School to join us, and Harvard's loss has been Canada's gain. The genius and inspiration of Dr. Tak Mak, Dr. David Jaffray, Dr. Jon Irish, Dr. Gary Rodin, Dr. John Dick, Dr. Neil Fleshner, Dr. Lillian Siu, Dr. Pamela Catton, and Dr. Malcolm Moore have contributed to the concept of passion capital. I would also like to thank and recognize all the members of the Princess Margaret Hospital Foundation for helping me learn the lessons of passion capital.

I'd like to thank my publisher, Doug Pepper of McClelland & Stewart, for his early and constant support. I would also like to thank my editors, Jenny Bradshaw and Kendra Ward, for their valuable and diligent editing.

Finally, I would like to thank Margo Clarke for her tireless support and encouragement as the manuscript came together.

SOURCES

1: DEFINING PASSION CAPITAL

Tracy Emin information taken from *The Telegraph*, August 20, 2011. Daniel Lanois material is from an interview (September 14, 2011), and from *Chronicles: Volume One*, Bob Dylan, pp. 181-220, Simon & Schuster. John Mackey is from *The New Yorker*, January 4, 2010; Statesman.com, December 19, 2009; *Opinion*, October 3, 2009.

2: CREED: THE POWER OF BELIEF

John D. Rockefeller material is from *Forbes Magazine*, February, 2008; *Titan: The Life of John D. Rockefeller, Sr.*, Ron Chernow, Warner Books; "Our History – A powerful legacy," rockefellerfoundation.org. Johnson & Johnson from *Reflections of Our Credo*; *Forbes Magazine*, "Airbnb's Tylenol moment," August 1, 2011; *Your Money*, "Tylenol made a hero of Johnson & Johnson: The recall that started them all," March 23, 2002. Henry Ford, *New York Times*, "Alan R. Mulally," January 28, 2011; *Wheels for the World: Henry Ford, His Company, and a Century of Progress*, Douglas Brinkley.

3: CULTURE: GROWING YOUR BELIEFS

Ken Thomson material from *Globe and Mail*, June 12, 2006; "What we need are more builders," Geoff Beattie, *Globe and Mail*, October 27, 2008. Isadore Sharp from *Four Seasons: The Story of a Business Philosophy*, Isadore Sharp. John F. Kennedy's inaugural address – www.bartleby.com. Easter Island material from A *Short History of Progress*, Ronald Wright, House of Anansi Press, 2004.

4: COURAGE: THE STRENGTH TO TAKE RISKS

Kathrine Switzer material from *Runner's World*, excerpting *Marathon Woman*, Kathrine Switzer, March 26, 2007. Bo Xilai from "Bo Xilai's 'red revival,'" *Globe and Mail*, May 7, 2011. Michael Jordan – "Failure" Nike commercial, YouTube, November 29, 2008. Baseball stats from franklyballpark.blogspot.com. George Soros is from *New York Times*, "A giver's agenda," December 17, 1996. Golda Meir is from *New York Times*, "Golda Meir: Peace and Arab Acceptance Were Goals of Her 5 Years as Premier," December 9, 1978. Michael Cohl is taken from "Satisfraction," *Saturday Night Magazine*, November, 1994.

5: BRAND: YOUR PROMISE TO THE WORLD

John Lasseter is taken from "Pixar's magic man," *Fortune*, May 17, 2006. Rolls Royce from Ogilvy.com. Oracle information from *The Economic Times*, "Oracle may exit software services business as part of plans to divest non-core assets," May 10, 2011. Steamwhistle taken from "Milestones in Steam Whistle Brewing History," www.steamwhistle.ca. Cirque du Soleil information – www.cirquedusoleil.com. Tata Motors is taken

from "India's Nano hits bumps on the road," *Globe and Mail*,
November 24, 2011; www.tatamotors.com. Wahaha Group is
from "The Chinese beverage company's expansion is no
laughing matter," *China Business Review*, September/
October, 2004; "Coke isn't it for China" *Forbes*, March 25,
2009; "Coca-Cola sees 'sustainable' China growth," *Financial
Times*, February 9, 2011; "Watch out, Coke and Pepsi – here
comes Wahaha," knowledge@Wharton, July 13, 2005. Mark
Burnett is from Life123.com, "Survivor the Reality TV Show
History"; Mark Burnett keynote speech, Realscreen conference, Washington, D.C. February, 2011. Own the Podium is
taken from ownthepodium.org.

6: RESOURCES: MARSHALLING AND MASTERING

George Bush and Hugo Chavez material comes from "Chavez:
'Bush has called me worse things,'" *Time Magazine*, September
22, 2006; "America the beautiful," *Walrus Magazine*, December/
January, 2006. Harry Rosen from www.harryrosen.com. Citibank
– "Citigroup tries to stop the drop in its share price," *New York
Times*, November 20, 2008. Gary Kurek from "For three
Canadian whiz kids, $100,000 and a goal: Change the world,"
Globe and Mail, May 26, 2011. Toronto demographics from CB
Richard Ellis Canada; "Suburbs lose out to the bright lights of
downtown," *Globe and Mail*, January 26, 2011. University of
Waterloo and Stanford material from "The heart of Silicon
Valley: Why Stanford – the nexus of capital, high technology,
and brainpower – is the intellectual incubator of the digital
age," *Fortune*, July 7, 1997; "The Invention of Waterloo," *Walrus
Magazine*, January, 2012. Chocolate information taken from
"My chocolate meltdown," *New York Times*, November 21,

2009. Robert Mondavi from www.decanter.com; *The House of Mondavi: The Rise and Fall of an American Wine Dynasty*, Julia Flynn Siler. T. Boone Pickens is taken from "High times for T. Boone Pickens," *Time Magazine*, March 4, 1985; boonepickens.com. Heinz Lehmann is from *In the Sleep Room*, Anne Collins. Craig Kielburger is from freethechildren. com; "Changing attitudes one T-shirt at a time," *Toronto Star*, October 16, 2008. Resource curse from "Natural Resource Abundance and Economic Growth," Jeffrey D. Sachs and Andrew M. Warner, Center for International Development and Harvard Institute for International Development.

7: STRATEGY: PLANNING WITH PASSION

ENIAC computer material is taken from *Popular Mechanics*, March, 1949. The Steve Jobs and Xerox information is from "Creation Myth," *The New Yorker*, May 16, 2011. Retirement statistics are from "Boomers Not Ready for Retirement: Survey" from *The Financial Post*, January 6, 2011; Harris/Decima poll; "Retirement 6/49," *Maclean's* magazine. Blockbuster material: "15 Companies That Might Not Survive 2009"; *U.S. News*; "Blockbuster to pull plug in Canada," *Globe and Mail*, August 31, 2011. Frederick Winslow Taylor: David Montgomery, *The Fall of the House of Labor: The Workplace, the State, and American Labor Activism* (1989), p. 251. Charles Bedaux: Steven Kreis, "The Diffusion of Scientific Management: The Bedaux Company in America and Britain, 1926–1945." Information on Dominic Barton came from an interview on August 30, 2011, and from his article "Capitalism for the long term," published in the *Harvard Business Review*, March 2011. Sunil Mittal: *Forbes Magazine*, "India's richest billionaires," November 18,

2009. TinePublic: "When Clinton and Bush come to town," *Globe and Mail, Report on Business*, November 9, 2009. Harlequin information is from "That old flame," *Walrus Magazine*, May, 2009. Generals Wolfe and Montcalm are from *Canada: A People's History* (2000), McClelland & Stewart. Bob Geldof: *Is That It?*, Penguin; Live 8 official website.

8: PERSISTENCE: IF AT FIRST YOU DON'T SUCCEED

Jay Walker material from "Browse the artifacts of geek history in Jay Walker's library," *Wired Magazine*, September 22, 2008; Encyclopedia of World Biography; "Jay Walker: The Priceline mogul races for new markets," *Business Week*, businessweek.com/ebiz. Insurance and Ping An material from TheHistoryOf.net, "The History of Insurance – Risk Through the Ages," March 28, 2011; IMD International, Perspectives for Managers, "The Making of an Insurance Giant," April, 2007. Sino-Forest taken from "Sino-Forest's worst enemy stands behind his report," *Globe and Mail*, June 9, 2011; "Sino-Forest hits back with documents; stock jumps," *Globe and Mail*, June 7, 2011; "A new note of caution takes its toll on Chinese stock listings," *Globe and Mail*, June 6, 2011. Geoff Beattie – "What we need are more builders," *Globe and Mail*, October 27, 2008. Sir Ronald Cohen from "Sir Ronald Cohen: Financier who is hoping for a peace dividend," *The Guardian*, July 7, 2006; "Let's hear those ideas," *The Economist*, August 14, 2010. Nelson Mandela from nobelprize.org; *Long Walk to Freedom*, Nelson Mandela, Little, Brown and Company. J.K. Rowling – "Famous Books Rejected Multiple Times, dailywritingtips.com; "J.K. Rowling and the Billion-Dollar Empire," *Forbes*, February 26, 2004. Cancer timeline – curetoday.com. Terry Fox – "Canada's

True Hero," *Maclean's Magazine*, July 5, 2004; *Terry Fox: His Story*, Leslie Scrivener, McClelland & Stewart.

9: MANAGEMENT AND LEADERSHIP: PUTTING PASSION TO WORK

Toronto Maple Leafs material taken from "Love among the ruins," *Saturday Night Magazine*, September, 1990; "History of Maple Leafs Ownership," *Globe and Mail*, December 9, 2011; *Years of Glory: 1942–1967*, edited by Dan Diamond, McClelland & Stewart. Montreal Canadiens material taken from "The Way They Win," *Vista Magazine*, March, 1989; *The Montreal Canadiens: An illustrated history of a hockey dynasty*, Claude Mouton, Key Porter. NHL valuations from "The business of hockey," *Forbes Magazine*, November 30, 2011. Football information from "Biggest first round quarterback busts," sports.yahoo.com, April 27, 2011; mynfldraft.com; nfl.com.

INDEX

ABOUT THE AUTHOR

PAUL ALOFS is an award-winning senior executive who has achieved extraordinary success in the retail, entertainment, Internet, marketing services, and social enterprise sectors.

After graduating from the University of Windsor in his hometown, Paul joined Colgate-Palmolive Canada in 1978. He obtained his MBA from York University in Toronto, and then worked with a marketing firm called the Marketing & Promotion Group. Pursuing a passion for music, Paul was named named President of HMV Music Stores Canada in 1989, where he increased the company's annual revenue from $30 million to over $200 million. Paul has also worked as an executive for the Walt Disney Company and MP3.com.

Paul was named one of Canada's Top 40 Under 40 business leaders in 1995. He has since been honoured by the University of Windsor with the Alumni Award of Merit and with an Honourary Ph.D. He has also received the Bryden Alumni Award from York University, and the Outstanding Progress and Achievement Award from the Schulich School of Business.

In addition to his extensive experience as an executive, Paul is also an active philanthropist and not-for-profit volunteer, having served as a board member for many organizations including Covenant House, Union for International Cancer Control, and Ozmosis Research, among others.

Since 2003, Paul has led The Princess Margaret Hospital Foundation, helping to raise $550 million for one of the world's top five cancer research centres.

Passion Capital: The World's Most Valuable Asset is his first book.